IN THE BEGINNING WAS THE WORD

Scriptures For The Lectionary
Speaking Choir, Cycle A

BY DALLAS A. BRAUNINGER

C.S.S. Publishing Co., Inc.
Lima, Ohio

IN THE BEGINNING WAS THE WORD

Library of Congress Cataloging-In-Publication Data

Bible. English. New Revised Standard. Selections. 1992.
In the beginning was the Word: scriptures for the lectionary speaking choir, Cycle A / [compiled] by Dallas A. Brauninger.
p.   cm.
Includes index.
ISBN 1-55673-437-9
1. Bible — Liturgical lessons, English. 2. Choral recitations. I. Brauninger, Dallas A., 1943-   . II. Title.
BV199.A2B73
264'.34—dc20   92-23729
                                                                                           CIP

9240 / ISBN 1-55673-437-9
            PRINTED IN U.S.A.

This volume is dedicated to
Ed and Ruth Haefele,
readers, listeners
and encouragers.

Table Of Contents

Preface

If you are interested in having the scripture come alive during a Sunday morning corporate service of worship, then these choral readings will aid you in the accomplishment of that goal. Dallas Brauninger's book takes one lectionary reading for each Sunday and other special days in the life of the church and develops them into a choral reading. Some readings involve only two people, and others take as many as eight or more. She suggests that they might be used as calls to worship, anthems, ordinary sequence with scripture reading, preface to pastoral prayer, or used in a story-telling fashion. You will find the scripture becomes alive as people share their voices and spirit in the reading of the Word.

These readings do not take a great deal of preparation time, yet that experience is a time of community-building. People really do learn to care for each other and appreciate each other in a new way. This is particularly true, for instance, if as a part of the choral reading group one person may be confined to a wheelchair. The mike is brought to this individual thus enabling one to be a part of the choral reading group. The intergenerational nature of the groups is supportive of who the church is called to be. Ideally, the more inter-cultural, inter-racial, intergenerational the group becomes, the more it is a microcosm of God's people.

The author is one who takes worship seriously and is always trying to find ways to make it more vital and meaningful. She is an individual who cares for humankind in an extraordinary manner. This is why she is so inclusive in the composition of the groups.

She has a feel for creation. Her daily walks bring her very close to God's creation and God's people. She is a biblical scholar who writes and creates out of the depths of a deep faith that has sustained her in the living of her own life. I have been with her many times and know her to be a person whose primary concern is the building of health and wholeness for humankind and creation. I like the way in which she makes many suggestions that causes one to think, dream and become creative.

I heartily commend this book to you and pray that it will be a blessing in your worship ministry.

Clarence "Clip" Higgins, Jr.

Introduction

These arrangements of scriptural choral readings include a cross section of assigned Psalms, first and second lessons and epistle readings from The Revised Common Lectionary: 1992. This book, the first of a proposed series of three, includes readings for Year A beginning with the first Sunday of Advent. This cycle repeats in 1995, 1998, 2001, 2004.

Purpose:
1. To hear the New Revised Standard Version of the Bible.
2. To attend more closely to the reading of scripture as a result of the assortment of voice choir arrangements.
3. To enjoy the variety of voices in your congregation.
4. To involve a wider number of people in worship.
5. To build community while preparing and reading together the selections.
6. To offer involvement and a blending of generations.
7. To offer participation in worship.
8. To give variety to calls to worship.
9. To provide occasional longer anthems as an addition to musical offerings.
10. To offer an expanded time of prayer with the "Before the Pastoral Prayer" meditative selections.

Guidelines:
Arrangements include a cross section of assigned Psalms, first and second lessons and epistle readings from The Revised Common Lectionary: 1992. The place in the service, and number and types of readers are suggested for each titled passage as well as a numbered reader key. Special instructions to readers in the text are underlined and set in parentheses, for example, *(Speak "Selah" softly as a spoken pause)."*

Tips For Voice Choir Readers:

1. Decide upon a standing order. Variety adds interest.
   - Stand in places at pews and turn with your back to as few people as possible.
   - Stand in a line by or in the chancel in the order of speakers or with the strongest voice in the middle. Some lay people may be more comfortable standing in the nave of the church in front of the pulpit or lectern than ascending the chancel steps.
   - For two-speaker readings, use the pulpit and lectern microphones.
   - Stand in a wide circle around the outside of the pews. The sound is outstanding with antiphonal readings or single speakers followed by the entire reading group.
   - Take a microphone to those who are not mobile so they can participate in a group reading.
   - Stand at the church narthex to offer a benediction reading.

2. To enable voices to carry, stand erect with weight distributed evenly between both feet. Breathe from the diaphragm rather than the upper chest. Relax your throat.

3. Locate a couple of people sitting toward the back. Speak directly to them. Speak with an attitude of having something special to tell them and of wanting them to hear the words clearly.

4. Keep your voice pitched slightly sharp rather than flat. A flat voice sounds tired. A slightly sharp pitch conveys interest and enthusiasm, inviting listening.

5. Words carry better if you hold up the text and keep your head up. It also helps to focus on shaping the words distinctly as you speak.

6. Enjoy reading the words. This is more important than reading with perfection. If you make a mistake, simply overlook it and continue reading.

7. Listen to other readers so you will stay together and follow a rhythm, as does a singing choir.

Reflections From A Participating Congregation:

Sunday our pastor held the microphone for Florence, a 90-year-old wheelchair-assisted woman who sits in the front pew so "I can hear everything." Florence and two other senior women read an arrangement of Psalm 100. With only a few words to read, Florence obviously enjoyed participating. When asked if she would like to do it again some time, she said with regret in her voice, "Oh, but I'll be gone next month to visit my sister."

These readings involve a wider number of people in worship. The only person in our congregation to decline an invitation to participate was a woman who could not yet manage her new bifocals. Another reader volunteered to be a last minute "fill-in any time." An eager first grader asked to read soon.

We arrange a month's schedule at a time giving readers the text beforehand. By stapling textsheets to construction paper, cutting off the top right corner and numbering the pages, we minimize confusion while reading.

Children tend to give a more polished reading when they practice a couple Sundays before their sharing. Other folk are comfortable with a one or two read-through practice before worship. Out of fairness to other readers, only those who practice participate in the reading during worship. This sometimes means assigning a second reading part to a confident reader. A little coaching offers encouragement and can bring about a solid reading.

We vary the use of the readings. Some are appropriate for the call to worship or expand the pastoral prayer. Others are suitable for the benediction or as a longer anthem.

The arranger of the readings designed them with certain members in mind: family members, disputing individuals, combinations of generations and those who simply need lifting up as creatures of God. Those regularly responsible for assigning readers for a particular selection may find that they, also, begin to "hear" the voices of certain individuals in the congregation as appropriate for a specific reading. In addition to positing a ministry of caring, preparing and reading the arrangements can enhance the building of community.

Advent 1
Psalm 122 (Psalm)
Peace Be Within You

Suggestions:
Use as an anthem.
2 readers — father and son

Key:
1 = man
2 = son

1:   I was glad when they said to me, "Let us go to the house of the Lord!"

2:   Our feet are standing within your gates, O Jerusalem. Jerusalem — built as a city that is bound firmly together.

1 and 2: To it the tribes go up,
the tribes of the Lord,
as was decreed for Israel,
to give thanks to the name of the Lord.

1:   For there the thrones for judgment were set up, the thrones of the house of David.

1 and 2: Pray for the peace of Jerusalem:

2:   "May they prosper who love you.

1:   Peace be within your walls,
and security within your towers."

2:   For the sake of my relatives and friends I will say, "Peace be within you."

1:   For the sake of the house of the Lord our God, I will seek your good.

Advent 2
Isaiah 11:1-10 (First Lesson)
The Peaceful Kingdom

Suggestions:
Use in ordinary sequence with the scripture reading.
2 readers — a couple

Key:
1 = female partner
2 = male partner

1: A shoot shall come out from the stump of Jesse,
and a branch shall grow out of his roots.

1 and 2: The spirit of the Lord shall rest on him,
the spirit of wisdom and understanding,
the spirit of counsel and might,
the spirit of knowledge and the fear of the Lord.

1: His delight shall be in the fear of the Lord.
He shall not judge by what his eyes see,
or decide by what his ears hear;

1 and 2: but with righteousness
he shall judge the poor,
and decide with equity
for the meek of the earth;
he shall strike the earth with the rod of his mouth,
and with the breath of his lips
he shall kill the wicked.

2: Righteousness shall be the belt around his waist, and
faithfulness the belt around his loins.

1 and 2: The wolf shall live with the lamb,
the leopard shall lie down with the kid,
the calf and the lion and the fatling together,
and a little child shall lead them.

1: The cow and the bear shall graze,
their young shall lie down together;
and the lion shall eat straw like the ox.

2: The nursing child shall play over the hole of the asp,
and the weaned child shall put its hand on the adder's den.

1 and 2: They will not hurt or destroy on all my holy mountain;
for the earth will be full of the knowledge of the Lord as the waters cover the sea.

1: On that day the root of Jesse
shall stand as a signal to the peoples;
the nations shall inquire of him,
and his dwelling shall be glorious.

Advent 3
Isaiah 35:1-10 (First Lesson)
The Holy Way

Suggestions:
Use as a call to worship.
6 readers — women of various ages

Key:
1-3 = higher voiced women
4-6 = deeper voiced women

1, 2, 3: The wilderness and the dry land shall be glad,
the desert shall rejoice and blossom;
like the crocus it shall blossom abundantly,
and rejoice with joy and singing.

4, 5, 6: The glory of Lebanon shall be given to it,
the majesty of Carmel and Sharon.

All: They shall see the glory of the Lord,
the majesty of our God.

1, 2, 3: Strengthen the weak hands,
and make firm the feeble knees.

All: Say to those who are of a fearful heart,
"Be strong, do not fear! Here is your God.
He will come with vengeance,
with terrible recompense.
He will come and save you."

1, 2, 3: Then the eyes of the blind shall be opened,
and the ears of the deaf unstopped;
then the lame shall leap like a deer,
and the tongues of the speechless sing for joy.

4, 5, 6: For waters shall break forth in the wilderness,
and streams in the desert;
the burning sand shall become a pool,
and the thirsty ground springs of water;
the haunt of jackals shall become a swamp,
the grass shall become reeds and rushes.

All: A highway shall be there,
and it shall be called the Holy Way;

1, 2, 3: the unclean shall not travel on it,
but it shall be for God's people;

1: no traveler,

2: not even fools,

1: shall go astray.

3: No lion shall be there,

1: nor shall any ravenous beast come up on it;

1, 2, 3: they shall not be found there,
but the redeemed shall walk there.

All: And the ransomed of the Lord shall return,
and come to Zion with singing;
everlasting joy shall be upon their heads;
they shall obtain joy and gladness,
and sorrow and sighing shall flee away.

Advent 4
Matthew 1:18-25 (Gospel Lesson)
The Birth Of Jesus

Suggestions:
Use in ordinary sequence with the scripture reading.
3 readers — women from three generations

Key:
1 = first storyteller
2 = second storyteller
3 = angel

1: Now the birth of Jesus the Messiah took place in this way. When his mother Mary had been engaged to Joseph, but before they lived together, she was found to be with child from the Holy Spirit.

2: Her husband Joseph, being a righteous man and unwilling to expose her to public disgrace, planned to dismiss her quietly. But just when he had resolved to do this, an angel of the Lord appeared to him in a dream and said,

3: "Joseph, son of David, do not be afraid to take Mary as your wife, for the child conceived in her is from the Holy Spirit. She will bear a son, and you are to name him Jesus, for he will save his people from their sins."

1: All this took place to fulfill what had been spoken by the Lord through the prophet: "Look, the virgin shall conceive and bear a son, and they shall name him Emmanuel," which means, "God is with us."

2: When Joseph awoke from sleep, he did as the angel of the Lord commanded him; he took her as his wife, but had no marital relations with her until she had borne a son; and he named him Jesus.

Christmas Eve/Christmas
Luke 2:1-14 (15-20) (Gospel Lesson)
The Birth Of Jesus

Suggestions:
Use in ordinary sequence with the scripture reading.
3 readers — women from three generations
* = optional stopping point

Key:
1 = first storyteller
2 = second storyteller
3 = angel

1:   In those days a decree went out from Emperor Augustus that all the world should be registered. This was the first registration and was taken while Quirinius was governor of Syria. All went to their own towns to be registered.

2:   Joseph also went from the town of Nazareth in Galilee to Judea, to the city of David called Bethlehem, because he was descended from the house and family of David. He went to be registered with Mary, to whom he was engaged and who was expecting a child.

1:   While they were there, the time came for her to deliver her child. And she gave birth to her firstborn son and wrapped him in bands of cloth, and laid him in a manger, because there was no place for them in the inn.

2:   In that region there were shepherds living in the fields, keeping watch over their flock by night. Then an angel of the Lord stood before them, and the glory of the Lord shone around them, and they were terrified. But the angel said to them,

3: "Do not be afraid; for see — I am bringing you good news of great joy for all the people: to you is born this day in the city of David a Savior, who is the Messiah, the Lord. This will be a sign for you: you will find a child wrapped in bands of cloth and lying in a manger."

1: And suddenly there was with the angel a multitude of the heavenly host, praising God and saying, "Glory to God in the highest heaven, and on earth peace among those whom he favors!"

*

2: When the angels had left them and gone into heaven, the shepherds said to one another, "Let us go now to Bethlehem and see this thing that has taken place, which the Lord has made known to us."

(2:) So they went with haste and found Mary and Joseph, and the child lying in the manger. When they saw this, they made known what had been told them about this child; and all who heard it were amazed at what the shepherds told them.

1: But Mary treasured all these words and pondered them in her heart.

2: The shepherds returned, glorifying and praising God for all they had heard and seen, as it had been told them.

Christmas 1
Matthew 2:13-23 (Gospel Lesson)
The Escape To Egypt
And The Return From Egypt

Suggestions:
Use as an anthem.
4 readers — 2 older women as storytellers, 2 middle-aged men

Key:
1 and 3 = storytellers
2 = angel
4 = prophet

1: Now after they had left, an angel of the Lord appeared to Joseph in a dream and said,

2: "Get up, take the child and his mother, and flee to Egypt, and remain there until I tell you; for Herod is about to search for the child, to destroy him."

1: Then Joseph got up, took the child and his mother by night, and went to Egypt, and remained there until the death of Herod.

3: This was to fulfill what had been spoken by the Lord through the prophet,

4: "Out of Egypt I have called my son."

1: When Herod saw that he had been tricked by the wise men, he was infuriated, and he sent and killed all the children in and around Bethlehem who were two years old or under, according to the time that he had learned from the wise men.

3: Then was fulfilled what had been spoken through the prophet Jeremiah:

4: "A voice was heard in Ramah, wailing and loud lamentation, Rachel weeping for her children; she refused to be consoled, because they are no more."

1: When Herod died, an angel of the Lord suddenly appeared in a dream to Joseph in Egypt and said,

2: "Get up, take the child and his mother, and go to the land of Israel, for those who were seeking the child's life are dead."

1: Then Joseph got up, took the child and his mother, and went to the land of Israel. But when he heard that Archelaus was ruling over Judea in place of his father Herod, he was afraid to go there. And after being warned in a dream, he went away to the district of Galilee.

3: There he made his home in a town called Nazareth, so that what had been spoken through the prophets might be fulfilled,

4: "He will be called a Nazorean."

Christmas 2
John 1:1-18 (Gospel Lesson)
In The Beginning Was The Word

Suggestions:
Use as an anthem or before the pastoral prayer.
5 readers — women
Voices 2-5 read in the manner of a softer, explaining chorus yet with a strength that affirms the words of the lead reader.

Key:
1 = lead reader, one with a matter-of-fact voice
2-5 = lighter pitched voices

1:   In the beginning was the Word,

2, 3, 4, 5: and the Word was with God,

2 and 3:   and the Word was God.

1:   He was in the beginning with God.

(1:)   All things came into being through him,

2, 3, 4, 5: and without him not one thing came into being.

1:   What has come into being in him was life,

2, 3, 4, 5: and the life was the light of all people.

2 and 3:   The light shines in the darkness,

4 and 5:   and the darkness did not overcome it.

(Read in storytelling fashion.)

`1:   There was a man sent from God, whose name was John. He came as a witness to testify to the light, so that all might believe through him.

2 and 3: He himself was not the light.

4 and 5: but he came to testify to the light.

1: The true light,

2, 3, 4, 5: which enlightens everyone,

1: was coming into the world.

(1:) He was in the world,

2, 3, 4, 5: and the world came into being through him;

1: yet the world did not know him.

(1:) He came to what was his own,

2, 3, 4, 5: and his own people did not accept him.

1: But to all who received him,

2, 3, 4, 5: who believed in his name,

1: he gave power to become children of God,

2 and 3: who were born, not of blood

3 and 4: or of the will of the flesh

4 and 5: or of the will of man,

2 and 3: but of God.

(1:) And the Word became flesh and lived among us,

2, 3, 4, 5: and we have seen his glory,
the glory as of a father's only son,
full of grace and truth.

5: (John testified to him and cried out, "This was he of whom I said, 'He who comes after me ranks ahead of me because he was before me.' ")

1: From his fullness we have all received,

2, 3, 4, 5: grace upon grace.

2 and 3: The law indeed was given through Moses;

4 and 5: grace and truth came through Jesus Christ.

1: No one has ever seen God.

2, 3, 4, 5: It is God the only Son,
who is close to the Father's heart,
who has made him known.

Epiphany
Isaiah 60:1-6 (First Lesson)
Glory Coming

Suggestions:
Use as a call to worship.
2 readers — men whose voice strengths are similar
Speak this duet with vigor.

Key:
1 = first reader
2 = second reader

1: Arise,

2: shine;

1 and 2: for your light has come,
and the glory of the Lord has risen upon you.

2: For darkness shall cover the earth,
and thick darkness the peoples;

1: but the Lord will arise upon you,

2: and his glory will appear over you.

1: Nations shall come to your light,
and kings to the brightness of your dawn.

(1:) Lift up your eyes and look around;

1 and 2: they all gather together,
they come to you;

2: your sons shall come from far away,

1: and your daughters shall be carried on their nurses' arms.

1 and 2: Then you shall see and be radiant; your heart shall thrill and rejoice,

2: because the abundance of the sea shall be brought to you, the wealth of the nations shall come to you.

1: A multitude of camels shall cover you, the young camels of Midian and Ephah; all those from Sheba shall come.

2: They shall bring gold and frankincense,

1 and 2: and shall proclaim the praise of the Lord.

Epiphany 1
Isaiah 42:1-9 (First Lesson)
The Lord's Servant

Suggestions:
Use in ordinary sequence with the scripture reading.
4 readers — men
Read this quartet with vigor.

Key:
1 and 2 = first readers
3 and 4 = second readers

1 and 2: Here is my servant, whom I uphold, my chosen,
in whom my soul delights;
I have put my spirit upon him;
he will bring forth justice to the nations.

3 and 4: He will not cry or lift up his voice, or make it heard
in the street;

3: a bruised reed he will not break,
and a dimly burning wick he will not quench;

4: he will faithfully bring forth justice.

3 and 4: He will not grow faint or be crushed until he has
established justice in the earth; and the coastlands
wait for his teaching.

1 and 2: Thus says God, the Lord,
who created the heavens and stretched them out,
who spread out the earth and what comes from it,
who gives breath to the people upon it
and spirit to those who walk in it:

3 and 4: I am the Lord,
I have called you in righteousness,
I have taken you by the hand and kept you;

3: I have given you as a covenant to the people,
a light to the nations,
to open the eyes that are blind,

4: to bring out the prisoners from the dungeon,
from the prison those who sit in darkness.

1 and 2: I am the Lord, that is my name;
my glory I give to no other,
nor my praise to idols.

3 and 4: See, the former things have come to pass,
and the new things I now declare;
before they spring forth, I tell you of them.

Epiphany 2
Psalm 40:1-11 (Psalm)
Let Your Steadfast Love And
Your Faithfulness Keep Me Safe Forever

Suggestions:
Use before the pastoral prayer.
4 readers — women

Key:
1 = deeper voice
2 = higher voice
3 = deeper voice
4 = higher voice

1: I waited patiently for the Lord;
he inclined to me and heard my cry.

2: He drew me up from the desolate pit,
out of the miry bog,
and set my feet upon a rock,
making my steps secure.

All: He put a new song in my mouth,
a song of praise to our God.

1: Many will see and fear,
and put their trust in the Lord.

2: Happy are those who make the Lord their trust,
who do not turn to the proud,
to those who go astray after false gods.

All: You have multiplied,
O Lord, my God,
your wondrous deeds and your thoughts toward us;
none can compare with you.

3: Were I to proclaim and tell of them,
they would be more than can be counted.

4: Sacrifice and offering you do not desire,
but you have given me an open ear.
Burnt offering and sin offering you have not required.

All: Then I said, "Here I am;
in the scroll of the book it is written of me.
I delight to do your will, O my God;
your law is within my heart."

3: I have told the glad news of deliverance
in the great congregation;
see, I have not restrained my lips,
as you know, O Lord.

4: I have not hidden your saving help within my heart,
I have spoken of your faithfulness and your salvation;
I have not concealed your steadfast love and your
faithfulness from the great congregation.

All: Do not, O Lord,
withhold your mercy from me;
let your steadfast love and your faithfulness keep
me safe forever.

Epiphany 3
Psalm 27:1, 4-9 (Psalm)
The Lord Is My Light And My Salvation

Suggestions:
Use before the pastoral prayer.
2 readers — a mature couple

Key:
1 = first reader
2 = second reader

1 and 2: The Lord is my light and my salvation;
whom shall I fear?
The Lord is the stronghold of my life;
of whom shall I be afraid?

1: One thing I asked of the Lord,
that will I seek after:
to live in the house of the Lord
all the days of my life,
to behold the beauty of the Lord,
and to inquire in his temple.

2: For he will hide me in his shelter
in the day of trouble;
he will conceal me under the cover of his tent;
he will set me high on a rock.

1: Now my head is lifted up above my enemies all
around me,
and I will offer in his tent sacrifices with shouts of
joy;

1 and 2: I will sing and make melody to the Lord.

1: Hear, O Lord, when I cry aloud,

2: be gracious to me and answer me!

1: "Come," my heart says, "seek his face!"
Your face, Lord, do I seek.
Do not hide your face from me.

1 and 2: Do not turn your servant away in anger,
you who have been my help.
Do not cast me off,
do not forsake me,
O God of my salvation!

Epiphany 4
Micah 6:1-8 (First Lesson)
What Does The Lord Require Of You?

Suggestions:
Read as an anthem.
4 readers — 2 men and 2 women

Key:
1 and 2 = men
3 and 4 = women

All: Hear what the Lord says:

1:   Rise, plead your case before the mountains,
and let the hills hear your voice.

2:   Hear, you mountains, the controversy of the Lord,
and you enduring foundations of the earth;

1:   for the Lord has a controversy with his people,
and he will contend with Israel.

3:   "O my people, what have I done to you?

4:   In what have I wearied you?

3 and 4:   Answer me!

3:   For I brought you up from the land of Egypt, and
redeemed you from the house of slavery;

4:   and I sent before you Moses, Aaron and Miriam.

3:   O my people, remember now what King Balak of
Moab devised, what Balaam son of Beor answered
him,

4:   and what happened from Shittim to Gilgal,

3 and 4: that you may know the saving acts of the Lord.''

All: ''With what shall I come before the Lord, and bow myself before God on high?

1:   Shall I come before him with burnt offerings, with calves a year old?
Will the Lord be pleased with thousands of rams, with tens of thousands of rivers of oil?

2:   Shall I give my firstborn for my transgression, the fruit of my body for the sin of my soul?''

All: He has told you, O mortal, what is good;
and what does the Lord require of you
but to do justice,
and to love kindness,
and to walk humbly with your God?

Epiphany 5
Matthew 5:13-16 (Gospel Lesson)
Two Sayings Of Jesus:
Salt Of The Earth And Light Of The World

Suggestions:
Use in ordinary sequence with the scripture reading.
2 readers — 2 men or 2 women

Key:
1 = stronger voice
2 = softer voice

1:   "You are the salt of the earth;

2:   but if salt has lost its taste, how can its saltiness be restored?
It is no longer good for anything, but is thrown out and trampled under foot.

1:   "You are the light of the world.

2:   A city built on a hill cannot be hid. No one after lighting a lamp puts it under the bushel basket, but on the lampstand, and it gives light to all in the house.

1:   In the same way, let your light shine before others, so that they may see your good works and give glory to your Father in heaven."

Epiphany 6
Matthew 5:17-26 (Gospel Lesson)
Sayings Of Jesus:
Jesus Comes To Fulfill The Law

Suggestions:
Use in ordinary sequence with the scripture reading.
9 readers — a variety of folk
Speakers read from a sitting position in their usual places in the pews.

Key:
1-9 = speakers

1: "Do not think I have come to abolish the law or the prophets; I have not come to abolish but to fulfill.

2: For truly I tell you, until heaven and earth pass away, not one letter, not one stroke of a letter, will pass from the law until all is accomplished.

3: Therefore, whoever breaks one of the least of these commandments, and teaches others to do the same, will be called least in the kingdom of heaven;

4: but whoever does them and teaches them will be called great in the kingdom of heaven.

5: For I tell you, unless your righteousness exceeds that of the scribes and Pharisees, you will never enter the kingdom of heaven.

6: "You have heard that it was said to those of ancient times, 'You shall not murder;' and 'whoever murders shall be liable to judgment.'

7: But I say to you that if you are angry with a brother or sister, you will be liable to judgment; and if you insult a brother or sister, you will be liable to the council; and if you say, 'You fool,' you will be liable to the hell of fire.

8: So when you are offering your gift at the altar, if you remember that your brother or sister has something against you, leave your gift there before the altar and go; first be reconciled to your brother or sister, and then come and offer your gift.

9: Come to terms quickly with your accuser while you are on the way to court with him, or your accuser may hand you over to the judge, and the judge to the guard, and you will be thrown into prison. Truly I tell you, you will never get out until you have paid the last penny.''

Epiphany 7
Matthew 5:38-48 (Gospel Lesson)
Teaching About Revenge And About Loving Enemies

Suggestions:
Use in ordinary sequence with the scripture reading.
10 speakers — men and women of all ages
Speakers read from a sitting position in usual places in the pews. If voices do not carry well in your sanctuary, invite speakers to sit near the center aisle and let the minister carry a portable microphone to each in an interviewing manner.

Key:
1-10 = readers

1: "You have heard that it was said, 'An eye for an eye and a tooth for a tooth.' But I say to you, Do not resist an evildoer. But if anyone strikes you on the right cheek, turn the other also;

2: and if anyone wants to sue you and take your coat, give your cloak as well;

3: and if anyone forces you to go one mile, go also the second mile.

4: Give to everyone who begs from you,

5: and do not refuse anyone who wants to borrow from you.

6: You have heard that it was said, 'You shall love your neighbor and hate your enemy.' But I say to you, Love your enemies and pray for those who persecute you, so that you may be children of your Father in heaven;

39

7: for he makes his sun rise on the evil and on the good, and sends rain on the righteousness and on the un-righteous.

8: For if you love those who love you, what reward do you have? Do not even the tax collectors do the same?

9: And if you greet only your brothers and sisters, what more are you doing than others? Do not even the gentiles do the same?

10: Be perfect, as your heavenly Father is perfect."

Epiphany 8
Psalm 131 (Psalm)
O Lord, My Heart Is Not Lifted Up

Suggestions:
Use before the pastoral prayer.
3 readers — women with serenity

Key:
1, 2, 3 = women

1: O Lord, my heart is not lifted up.

2: my eyes are not raised too high;

1: I do not occupy myself with things
too great and too marvelous for me.

3: But I have calmed and quieted my soul,
like a weaned child with its mother;

2: my soul is like the weaned child that is with me.

All: O Israel, hope in the Lord from this time on and
forevermore.

Transfiguration Sunday
Matthew 17:1-9 (Gospel Lesson)
The Transfiguration

Suggestions:
Use in ordinary sequence with the scripture reading.
4 readers — 2 women (1 as God), 2 men

Key:
1 = storyteller
2 = Peter
3 = God
4 = Jesus

1:   Six days later, Jesus took with him Peter and James and his brother John and led them up a high mountain, by themselves.

(1:)   And he was transfigured before them, and his clothes became dazzling white. Suddenly there appeared to them Moses and Elijah, talking with him. Then Peter said to Jesus,

2:   "Lord, it is good for us to be here; if you wish, I will make three dwellings here, one for you, one for Moses, and one for Elijah."

1:   While he was still speaking, suddenly a bright cloud overshadowed them, and from the cloud a voice said,

3:   "This is my Son, the Beloved; with him I am well pleased; listen to him!"

1:   When the disciples heard this, they fell to the ground and were overcome by fear. But Jesus came and touched them, saying,

4:   "Get up and do not be afraid."

1:   And when they looked up, they saw no one except Jesus himself alone. As they were coming down the mountain, Jesus ordered them,

4:   "Tell no one about the vision until after the Son of Man has been raised from the dead."

Ash Wednesday
Psalm 51:1-17 (Psalm)
Create In Me A Clean Heart, O God

Suggestions:
Use as a prayer.
Read from a sitting position from usual place in the pews.
14 readers — a variety of folk

Key:
1 14 = readers

1:      Have mercy on me, O God, according to your stead-fast love;

2:      according to your abundant mercy blot out my transgressions.

3:      Wash me thoroughly from my iniquity, and cleanse me from my sin.

4:      For I know my transgressions, and my sin is ever before me.

5:      Against you, you alone, have I sinned, and done what is evil in your sight, so that you are justified in your sentence and blameless when you pass judgment.

6:      Indeed, I was born guilty, a sinner when my mother conceived me.

7:      You desire truth in the inward being; therefore teach me wisdom in my secret heart.

8:      Purge me with hyssop, and I shall be clean; wash me, and I shall be whiter than snow.

9: Let me hear joy and gladness; let the bones that you have crushed rejoice.

10: Hide your face from my sins, and blot out all my iniquities.

All: Create in me a clean heart, O God, and put a new and right spirit within me.

11: Do not cast me away from your presence, and do not take your holy spirit from me.

All: Restore to me the joy of your salvation, and sustain in me a willing spirit.

12: Then I will teach transgressors your ways, and sinners will return to you.

13: Deliver me from bloodshed, O God, O God of my salvation, and my tongue will sing aloud of your deliverance.

All: O Lord, open my lips,
and my mouth will declare your praise.

14: For you have no delight in sacrifice; if I were to give a burnt offering, you would not be pleased. The sacrifice acceptable to God is a broken spirit; a broken and contrite heart, O God, you will not despise.

Lent 1
Matthew 4:1-11 (Gospel)
The Temptation Of Jesus

Suggestions:
Use in ordinary sequence with the scripture reading.
3 readers — 1 younger woman, 1 older woman, 1 young man

Key:
1 = storyteller
2 = tempter
3 = Jesus

1: Then Jesus was led up by the Spirit into the wilderness to be tempted by the devil. He fasted 40 days and 40 nights, and afterwards he was famished. The tempter came and said to him,

2: "If you are the Son of God, command these stones to become loaves of bread."

1: But he answered,

3: "It is written, 'One does not live by bread alone, but by every word that comes from the mouth of God.' "

1: Then the devil took him to the holy city and placed him on the pinnacle of the temple, saying to him,

2: "If you are the Son of God, throw yourself down; for it is written, 'He will command his angels concerning you,' and 'On their hands they will bear you up, so that you will not dash your foot against a stone.' "

1: Jesus said to him,

3: "Again it is written, 'Do not put the Lord your God to the test.' "

1: Again, the devil took him to a very high mountain and showed him all the kingdoms of the world and their splendor; and he said to him,

2: "All these I will give you, if you will fall down and worship me."

1: Jesus said to him,

3: "Away with you, Satan! for it is written, 'Worship the Lord your God, and serve only him.' "

1: Then the devil left him, and suddenly angels came and waited on him.

Lent 2
Psalm 121 (Psalm)
I Lift Up My Eyes To The Hills

Suggestions:
Use before the pastoral prayer.
2 readers — senior spouses

Key:
1 = man
2 = woman

1: I lift up my eyes to the hills —
from where will my help come?

2: My help comes from the Lord,
who made heaven and earth.

1 and 2: He will not let your foot be moved;
he who keeps you will not slumber.
He who keeps Israel
will neither slumber nor sleep.

2: The Lord is your keeper;
the Lord is your shade at your right hand.

1: The sun shall not strike you by day,
nor the moon by night.

2: The Lord will keep you from all evil;

1: he will keep your life.

1 and 2: The Lord will keep your going out and your coming in from this time on and forevermore.

Lent 3
John 4:5-42 (Gospel Lesson)
Jesus And The Woman Of Samaria

Suggestions:
Use as an anthem.
4 readers — 2 women, 2 men (second storyteller should have a soft voice)

Key:
1 = first storyteller
2 = second storyteller
3 = Jesus
4 = Samaritan woman

1:   So [Jesus] came to a Samaritan city called Sychar, near the plot of ground that Jacob had given to his son Joseph. Jacob's well was there, and Jesus, tired out by his journey, was sitting by the well.

(1:)   It was about noon. A Samaritan woman came to draw water, and Jesus said to her,

3:   "Give me a drink."

(Speak as an aside.)
2:   (His disciples had gone to the city to buy food.)

1   The Samaritan woman said to him,

4:   "How is it that you, a Jew, ask a drink of me, a woman of Samaria?"

(Speak as an aside.)
2:   (Jews do not share things in common with Samaritans.)

49

1: Jesus answered her,

3: "If you knew the gift of God, and who it is that is saying to you, 'Give me a drink,' you would have asked him, and he would have given you living water."

1: The woman said to him,

4: "Sir, you have no bucket, and the well is deep. Where do you get that living water? Are you greater than our ancestor Jacob, who gave us the well, and with his sons and his flocks drank from it?"

1: Jesus said to her,

3: "Everyone who drinks of this water will be thirsty again, but those who drink of the water that I will give them will never be thirsty. The water that I will give will become in them a spring of water gushing up to eternal life."

1: The woman said to him,

4: "Sir, give me this water, so that I may never be thirsty or have to keep coming here to draw water."

1: Jesus said to her,

3: "Go, call your husband, and come back."

1: The woman answered him,

4: "I have no husband."

1: Jesus said to her,

3: "You are right in saying, 'I have no husband'; for you have had five husbands, and the one you have now is not your husband. What you have said is true!"

1: The woman said to him,

4: "Sir, I see that you are a prophet. Our ancestors worshiped on this mountain, but you say that the place where people must worship is in Jerusalem."

1: Jesus said to her,

3: "Woman, believe me, the hour is coming when you will worship the Father neither on this mountain nor in Jerusalem. You worship what you do not know; we worship what we know, for salvation is from the Jews.

(3:) But the hour is coming, and is now here, when the true worshipers will worship the Father in spirit and truth, for the Father seeks such as these to worship him. God is spirit, and those who worship him must worship in spirit and truth."

1: The woman said to him,

4: "I know that Messiah is coming"

(Speak as an aside.)
2: (who is called Christ).

4: "When he comes, he will proclaim all things to us."

1: Jesus said to her,

3: "I am he, the one who is speaking to you."

1: Just then his disciples came. They were astonished that he was speaking with a woman, but no one said, "What do you want?" or, "Why are you speaking with her?" Then the woman left her water jar and went back to the city. She said to the people,

4: "Come and see a man who told me everything I have ever done! He cannot be the Messiah, can he?"

1: They left the city and wee on their way to him. Meanwhile the disciples were urging him, "Rabbi, eat something." But he said to them,

3: "I have food to eat that you do not know about."

1: So the disciples said to one another, "Surely no one has brought him something to eat?" Jesus said to them,

3: "My food is to do the will of him who sent me and to complete his work. Do you not say, 'Four months more, then comes the harvest?' But I tell you, look around you, and see how the fields are ripe for harvesting.

(3:) The reaper is already receiving wages and is gathering fruit for eternal life, so that sower and reaper may rejoice together. For here the saying holds true, 'One sows and another reaps.' I sent you to reap that for which you did not labor. Others have labored, and you have entered into their labor."

1: Many Samaritans from that city believed in him because of the woman's testimony, "He told me everything I have ever done." So when the Samaritans came to him, they asked him to stay with them; and he stayed there two days. And many more believed because of his word.

(1:) They said to the woman, "It is no longer because of what you said that we believe, for we have heard for ourselves, and we know that this is truly the Savior of the world."

Lent 4
John 9:1-41 (Gospel)
Jesus Heals The Blind Man

Suggestions:
Use as an anthem.
5 readers — 1 woman as storyteller, 4 men

Key:
1 = storyteller
2 = disciple
3 = Jesus
4 = the healed man
5 = parent of the healed man

1: As he walked along, he saw a man blind from birth. His disciples asked him,

2: "Rabbi, who sinned, this man or his parents, that he was born blind?"

1: Jesus answered:

3: "Neither this man nor his parents sinned; he was born blind so that God's works might be revealed in him. We must work the works of him who sent me while it is day; night is coming when no one can work. As long as I am in the world, I am the light of the world."

1: When he had said this, he spat on the ground and made mud with the saliva and spread the mud on the man's eyes, saying to him,

3: "Go, wash in the pool of Siloam"

1: (which means Sent). Then he went and washed and came back able to see. The neighbors and those who had seen him before as a beggar began to ask, "Is this not the man who used to sit and beg?'' Some were saying, ''It is he.'' Others were saying, ''No, but it is someone like him.'' He kept saying,

4: ''I am the man.''

1: But they kept asking him, ''Then how were your eyes opened?'' He answered,

4: ''The man called Jesus made mud, spread it on my eyes, and said to me, 'Go to Siloam and wash.' Then I went and washed and received my sight.''

1: They said to him, ''Where is he?'' He said,

4: ''I do not know.''

1: They brought to the Pharisees the man who had formerly been blind. Now it was a sabbath day when Jesus made the mud and opened his eyes. Then the Pharisees also began to ask him how he had received his sight. He said to them,

4: ''He put mud on my eyes. Then I washed, and now I see.''

1: Some of the Pharisees said, ''This man is not from God, for he does not observe the sabbath.'' But others said, ''How can a man who is a sinner perform such signs?'' And they were divided. So they said again to the blind man, ''What do you say about him? It was your eyes he opened.'' He said,

4: ''He is a prophet.''

1: The Jews did not believe that he had been blind and he had received his sight until they called the parents of the man who had received his sight and asked them, ''Is this your son, who you say was born blind? How then does he now see?" His parents answered,

5: "We know that this is our son, and that he was born blind; but we do not know how it is that now he sees, nor do we know who opened his eyes. Ask him; he is of age. He will speak for himself."

1: His parents said this because they were afraid of the Jews; for the Jews had already agreed that anyone who confessed Jesus to be the Messiah would be put out of the synagogue. Therefore his parents said,

5: "He is of age; ask him."

1: So for the second time they called the man who had been blind, and they said to him, "Give glory to God! We know that this man is a sinner." He answered,

4: "I do not know whether he is a sinner. One thing I do know, that though I was blind, now I see."

1: They said to him, "What did he do to you? How did he open your eyes?" He answered them,

4: "I have told you already, and you would not listen. Why do you want to hear it again? Do you also want to become his disciples?"

1: Then they reviled him, saying, "You are his disciple, but we are disciples of Moses. We know that God has spoken to Moses, but as for this man, we do not know where he comes from." The man answered,

4: "Here is an astonishing thing! You do not know where he comes from, and yet he opened my eyes. We know that God does not listen to sinners, but he does listen to one who worships him and obeys his will. Never since the world began has it been heard that anyone opened the eyes of a person born blind. If this man were not from God, he could do nothing.''

1: They answered him, ''You were born entirely in sins, and are you trying to teach us?'' And they drove him out. Jesus heard that they had driven him out, and when he found him, he said,

3: ''Do you believe in the Son of Man?''

1: He answered,

4: ''And who is he, sir? Tell me, so that I may believe in him.''

1: Jesus said to him,

3: ''You have seen him, and the one speaking with you is he.''

1: He said,

4: ''Lord, I believe.''

1: And he worshiped him. Jesus said,

3: ''I came into this world for judgment so that those who do not see may see, and those who do see may become blind.''

1: Some of the Pharisees near him heard this and said to him, ''Surely we are not blind, are we?'' Jesus said to them,

3: ''If you were blind, you would not have sin. But now that you say, 'We see,' your sin remains.''

Lent 5
Ezekiel 37:1-14 (First Lesson)
The Valley Of Dry Bones

Suggestions:
Use as an anthem.
2 readers — men with strong voices
In this spoken duet, contrast an energetic and amazed Ezekiel
with a matter-of-fact Lord.

Key:
1 = Ezekiel
2 = The Lord

1: The hand of the Lord came upon me, and he brought me out of the spirit of the Lord and set me down in the middle of a valley; it was full of bones. He led me all around them; there were very many lying in the valley, and they were very dry. He said to me,

2: "Mortal, can these bones live?"

1: I answered, "O Lord God, you know." Then he said to me,

2: "Prophesy to these bones, and say to them: O dry bones, hear the word of the Lord. Thus says the Lord God to these bones: I will cause breath to enter you, and you shall live.

(2:) I will lay sinews on you, and will cause flesh to come upon you, and cover you with skin, and put breath in you, and you shall live; and you shall know that I am the Lord."

1: So I prophesied as I had been commanded; and as I prophesied, suddenly there was a noise, a rattling, and the bones came together, bone to its bone. I looked, and there were sinews on them, and flesh had come upon them, and skin had covered them; but there was no breath in them. Then he said to me,

2: "Prophesy to the breath, prophesy, mortal, and say to the breath: Thus says the Lord God: Come from the four winds, O breath, and breathe upon these slain, that they may live."

1: I prophesied as he commanded me, and the breath came into them, and they lived, and stood on their feet, a vast multitude. Then he said to me,

2: "Mortal, these bones are on the whole house of Israel. They say, 'Our bones are dried up, and our hope is lost; we are cut off completely.' Therefore prophesy, and say to them,

(2:) Thus says the Lord God: I am going to open your graves, and bring you up from your graves, O my people; and I will bring you back to the land of Israel. And you shall know that I am the Lord, when I open your graves, and bring you up from your graves, O my people.

(2:) I will put my spirit within you, and you shall live, and I will place you on your own soil; then you shall know that I, the Lord, have spoken and will act,"

1: says the Lord.

Palm Sunday
Philippians 2:5-11 (Second Lesson)
The Attitude Of Christ

Suggestions:
Use before the pastoral prayer.
3 readers — all women

Key:
1 = deeper voice
2 = medium voice
3 = higher voice

1: Let the same mind be in you that was in Christ Jesus, who,

2: though he was in the form of God,

3: did not regard equality with God as something to be exploited,

2: but emptied himself, taking the form of a slave,

3: being born in human likeness.

1: And being found in human form, he humbled himself and became obedient to the point of death —

2: even death on a cross.

1: Therefore God also highly exalted him

2: and gave him the name that is above every name,

All: so that at the name of Jesus every knee should bend,

1: in heaven

2 and 3: and on earth

All: and under the earth,

1: and every tongue should confess that Jesus Christ is Lord,

All: to the glory of God the Father.

Holy Week — Monday
Psalm 36:1, 5-11 (Psalm)
God's Steadfast Love

Suggestions:
Use as one segment of a Palm Sunday stations of the cross service where each day of Holy Week is lifted up.
Use in a newsletter for family meditation during Holy Week.
4 readers — a combination of two or three generations
If read by one person, pause to meditate after each numbered section. If read by two people, alternate sections.

Key:
1 = first reader
2 = second reader
3 = third reader
4 = fourth reader

1: Transgression speaks to the wicked deep in their hearts;

All: there is no fear of God before their eyes.

2: Your steadfast love, O Lord, extends to the heavens, your faithfulness to the clouds.

3: Your righteousness is like the mighty mountains, your judgments are like the great deep; you save humans and animals alike, O Lord.

All: How precious is your steadfast love, O God!

4: All people may take refuge in the shadow of your wings.

3: They feast on the abundance of your house, and you give them drink from the river of your delights.

61

1: For with you is the fountain of life; in your light we see light.

All: O continue your steadfast love to those who know you, and your salvation to the upright of heart!

2: Do not let the foot of the arrogant tread on me, or the hand of the wicked drive me away.

Holy Week — Tuesday
Psalm 71:1-16 (Psalm)
In You, O God, I Take Refuge

Suggestions:
Use as one segment of a Palm Sunday stations of the cross
service where each day of Holy Week is lifted up.
Use in a newsletter for family meditation during Holy Week.
4 readers — a combination of two or three generations
If read by one person, pause to meditate after each numbered
section. If read by two people, alternate sections.

Key:
1 = first reader
2 = second reader
3 = third reader
4 = fourth reader

1:   In you, O Lord, I take refuge; let me never be put
to shame.

All: In your righteousness deliver me and rescue me; in-
cline your ear to me and save me.

2:   Be to me a rock of refuge, a strong fortress, to save
me, for you are my rock and my fortress. Rescue
me, O my God, from the hand of the wicked, from
the grasp of the unjust and cruel.

3:   For you, O Lord, are my hope,
my trust, O Lord, from my youth.

4:   Upon you I have leaned from my birth; it was you
who took me from my mother's womb.

All: My praise is continually of you.

2: I have been like a portent to many, but you are my strong refuge.

All: My mouth is filled with your praise, and with your glory all day long.

4: Do not cast me off in the time of old age; do not forsake me when my strength is spent.

2: For my enemies speak concerning me, and those who watch for my life consult together. They say, "Pursue and seize that person whom God has forsaken, for there is no one to deliver."

All: O God, do not be far from me;
O my God, make haste to help me!

4: Let my accusers be put to shame and consumed; let those who seek to hurt me be covered with scorn and disgrace.

3: But I will hope continually,
and will praise you yet more and more.

2: My mouth will tell of your righteous acts, of your deeds of salvation all day long, though their number is past my knowledge.

1: I will come praising the mighty deeds of the Lord God, I will praise your righteousness, yours alone.

Holy Week — Wednesday
Psalm 70 (Psalm)
God, You Are My Help And Deliverer

Suggestions:
Use as one segment of a Palm Sunday stations of the cross service where each day of Holy Week is lifted up.
Use in a newsletter for family meditation during Holy Week.
4 readers — a combination of two or three generations
If read by one person, pause to meditate after each numbered section. If read by two people, alternate sections.

Key:
1 = first reader
2 = second reader
3 = third reader
4 = fourth reader

All: Be pleased, O God, to deliver me.
O Lord, make haste to help me!

1: Let those be put to shame and confusion who seek my life.

2: Let those be turned back and brought to dishonor who desire to hurt me.

3: Let those who say, "Aha, Aha!" turn back because of their shame.

All: Let all who seek you rejoice and be glad in you.

1: Let those who love your salvation say evermore, "God is great!"

2: But I am poor and needy; hasten to me, O God!

All: You are my help and my deliverer; O Lord, do not delay!

Holy Week — Maundy Thursday
Psalm 116:1-2, 12-19 (Psalm)
I Will Pay My Vows To The Lord

Suggestions:
Use as a call to worship.
Use as one segment of a Palm Sunday stations of the cross service where each day of Holy Week is lifted up.
Use in a newsletter for family meditation during Holy Week.
4 readers — a combination of two or three generations
If read by one person, pause to meditate after each numbered section. If read by two people, alternate sections.

Key:
1 = first reader
2 = second reader
3 = third reader
4 = fourth reader

1: I love the Lord, because he has heard my voice and my supplications.

All: Because he inclined his ear to me, therefore I will call on him as long as I live.

2: What shall I return to the Lord for all his bounty to me?

All: I will lift up the cup of salvation
and call on the name of the Lord,
I will pay my vows to the Lord in the presence of all his people.

3: Precious in the sight of the Lord is the death of his faithful ones.

All: O Lord, I am your servant; I am your servant, the child of your serving girl.

4:   You have loosed my bonds.
I will offer to you a thanksgiving sacrifice and call
on the name of the Lord.

All: I will pay my vows to the Lord
in the presence of all his people,
in the courts of the house of the Lord,
in your midst, O Jerusalem.
Praise the Lord!

Holy Week — Good Friday
Psalm 22 (Psalm)
My God, Why Have You Forsaken Me?

Suggestions:
Use as an anthem.
Use as one segment of a Palm Sunday stations of the cross
service where each day of Holy Week is lifted up.
Use in a newsletter for family meditation during Holy Week.
4 readers — a combination of two or three generations
If read by one person, pause to meditate after each numbered
section. If read by two people, alternate sections.

Key:
1 = first reader
2 = second reader
3 = third reader
4 = fourth reader

All: My God, my God, why have you forsaken me?
Why are you so far from helping me,
from the words of my groaning?

1: O my God, I cry by day, but you do not answer;
and by night, but find no rest.

All: Yet you are holy,
enthroned on the praises of Israel.
In you our ancestors trusted;
they trusted, and you delivered them.

2: To you they cried, and were saved;
in you they trusted,
and were not put to shame.

All: But I am a worm, and not human;
scorned by others,
and despised by the people.

3: All who see me mock at me;
they make mouths at me,
they shake their heads;

All: "Commit your cause to the Lord;
let him deliver —
let him rescue the one in whom he delights!"

4: Yet it was you who took me from the womb;
you kept me safe on my mother's breast.
On you I was cast from my birth,
and since my mother bore me you have been my
God.

All: Do not be far from me,
for trouble is near and there is no one to help.

1: Many bulls encircle me,
strong bulls of Bashan surround me;
they open wide their mouths at me,
like a ravening and roaring lion.

2: I am poured out like water,
and all my bones are out of joint;
my heart is like wax;
it is melted within my breast;
my mouth is dried up like a potsherd,
and my tongue sticks to my jaws;
you lay me in the dust of death.

3: For dogs are all around me;
a company of evildoers encircles me.
My hands and feet have shriveled;
I can count all my bones.
They stare and gloat over me;
They divide my clothes among themselves,
and for my clothing they cast lots.

All: But you, O Lord, do not be far away!
O my help, come quickly to my aid!

3: Deliver my soul from the sword,
my life from the power of the dog!
Save me from the mouth of the lion!
From the horns of the wild oxen you have rescued
me.

4: I will tell of your name to my brothers and sisters;
In the midst of the congregation I will praise you:

All: You who fear the Lord, praise him!
All you offspring of Jacob, glorify him;
stand in awe of him,
all you offspring of Israel!

2: For he did not despise or abhor the affliction of the
afflicted;
he did not hide his face from me,
but heard when I cried to him.

1: From you comes my praise in the great
congregation;
my vows I will pay before those who fear him.

4: The poor shall eat and be satisfied;
those who seek him shall praise the Lord.

All: May your hearts live forever!

3: All the ends of the earth shall remember and turn
to the Lord;
and all the families of the nations shall worship before him.

All: For dominion belongs to the Lord,
and he rules over the nations.

1: To him, indeed, shall all who sleep in the earth bow down;
before him shall bow all who go down to the dust,
and I shall live for him.
Posterity will serve him;
future generations will be told about the Lord,
and proclaim his deliverance to a people yet
unborn, saying that he has done it.

Holy Week — Holy Saturday
Psalm 31:1-4, 15-16 (Psalm)
A Prayer Of Trust In God

Suggestions:
Use as one segment of a Palm Sunday stations of the cross service where each day of Holy Week is lifted up.
Use in a newsletter for family meditation during Holy Week.
4 readers — a combination of two or three generations
If read by one person, pause to meditate after each numbered section. If read by two people, alternate sections.

Key:
1 = first reader
2 = second reader
3 = third reader
4 = fourth reader

1:   In you, O Lord, I seek refuge;
         do not let me ever be put to shame;

2:   in your righteousness deliver me.
         Incline your ear to me;
         rescue me speedily.

3:   Be a rock of refuge for me,
         a strong fortress to save me.

4:   You are indeed my rock and my fortress;
         for your name's sake lead me and guide me,

3:   take me out of the net that is hidden for me,
         for you are my refuge.

2: My times are in your hand;
deliver me from the hand of my enemies and
persecutors.

4: Let your face shine upon your servant;
save me in your steadfast love.

Easter
Colossians 3:1-4 (Second Lesson)
Raised With Christ

Suggestions:
Use as a call to worship or as a benediction.
2 readers — 2 men

Key:
1 = deeper voice
2 = tenor voice

1: So if you have been raised with Christ,
seek the things that are above,
where Christ is,
seated at the right hand of God.

2: Set your minds on things that are above,
not on things that are on earth,
for you have died,
and your life is hidden with Christ in God.

1: When Christ who is your life is revealed,
then you also will be revealed with him in glory.

Easter 2
1 Peter 1:3-9 (Second Lesson)
The Living Hope

Suggestions:
Use in ordinary sequence with the scripture reading.
4 readers — 2 long-married couples

Key:
1 and 2 = first couple
3 and 4 = second couple

All: Blessed be the God and Father of our Lord Jesus Christ!

1: By his great mercy he has given us a new birth

2: into a living hope through the resurrection of Jesus Christ from the dead,

1: and into an inheritance that is imperishable,

2: undefiled, and unfading,

1: kept in heaven for you, who are being protected by the power of God through faith

2: for a salvation ready to be revealed in the last time.

3: In this you rejoice,

4: even if now for a little while you have had to suffer various trials,

3: so that the genuineness of your faith

4:   — being more precious than gold that, though
perishable, is tested by fire —

3:   may be found to result in praise and glory and honor
when Jesus Christ is revealed.

1:   Although you have not seen him,
you love him;

2:   and even though you do not see him now,

3:   you believe in him and rejoice with an
indescribable and glorious joy.

4:   for you are receiving the outcome of your faith,
the salvation of your souls.

Easter 3
1 Peter 1:17-23 (Second Lesson)
Loving Deeply From The Heart

Suggestions:
Use in ordinary sequence with the scripture reading.
3 readers — men or women

Key:
1 = first reader
2 = second reader
3 = third reader

1: If you invoke as Father the one who judges all people impartially according to their deeds,

2: live in reverent fear during the time of your exile.

1: You know that you were ransomed from the futile ways inherited from your ancestors,

2: not with perishable things like silver or gold,

3: but with the precious blood of Christ, like that of a lamb without defect or blemish.

1: He was destined before the foundation of the world,

2: but was revealed at the end of the ages for your sake.

3: Through him you have come to trust in God, who raised him from the dead and gave him glory, so that your faith and hope are set on God.

1: Now that you have purified your souls by your obedience to the truth so that you have genuine mutual love,

3:   love one another deeply from the heart.

1:   You have been born anew,

2:   not of perishable but of imperishable seed,

1:   through the living and enduring word of God.

Easter 4
Psalm 23 (Psalm)
The Lord Is My Shepherd

Suggestions:
Use before the pastoral prayer.
6 readers — males spanning three generations
Read from usual position in pew.
Read with an attitude of pondering aloud yet with a voice which
can be heard.

Key:
Readers from 1 to 6 in descending age order

1:       The Lord is my shepherd, I shall not want.
He makes me lie down in green pastures;
he leads me beside still waters;

5:       he restores my soul.
He leads me in right paths for his name's sake.

4:       Even though I walk through the darkest valley,
I fear no evil;
for you are with me.

2:       your rod and your staff — they comfort me.

All: You prepare a table before me in the presence of
my enemies;
you anoint my head with oil; my cup overflows.

6:       Surely goodness and mercy shall follow me all the
days of my life,

3:       and I shall dwell in the house of the Lord my whole
life long.

Easter 5
John 14:1-14 (Gospel)
In My Father's House

Suggestions:
Use before the pastoral prayer.
4 readers — 3 boys, 1 girl

Key:
1 = Jesus
2 = storyteller
3 = Thomas
4 - Phillip

1: "Do not let your hearts be troubled. Believe in God, believe also in me. In my Father's house there are many dwelling places. If it were not so, would I have told you that I go to prepare a place for you?

(1:) And if I go and prepare a place for you, I will come again and will take you to myself, so that where I am, there you may be also. And you know the way to the place where I am going."

2: Thomas said to him,

3: "Lord, we do not know where you are going. How can we know the way?"

2: Jesus said to him,

1: "I am the way, and the truth and the life. No one comes to the Father except through me. If you know me, you will know my Father also. From now on you do know him and have seen him."

2: Philip said to him,

4: "Lord, show us the Father, and we will be satisfied."

2: Jesus said to him,

1: "Have I been with you all this time, Philip, and you still do not know me? Whoever has seen me has seen the Father. How can you say, 'Show us the Father'? Do you not believe that I am in the Father and the Father is in me?

(1:) The words that I say to you I do not speak on my own; but the Father who dwells in me does his works. Believe me that I am in the Father and the Father is in me; but if you do not, then believe me because of the works themselves.

(1:) Very truly, I tell you, the one who believes in me will also do the works that I do and, in fact, will do greater works than these, because I am going to the Father. I will do whatever you ask in my name, so that the Father may be glorified in the Son. If in my name you ask me for anything, I will do it."

Easter 6
1 Peter 3:13-22 (Second Lesson)
Living As A Christian

Suggestions:
Use in ordinary sequence with the scripture reading.
Speakers read from a sitting position in their usual places in the pews in an informal advice-offering manner.
7 readers — various ages

Key:
1-7 = speakers

1:   Now who will harm you if you are eager to do what is good? But even if you do suffer for doing what is right, you are blessed.

2:   Do not fear what they fear, and do not be intimidated, but in your hearts sanctify Christ as Lord.

3:   Always be ready to make your defense to anyone who demands from you an accounting for the hope that is in you; yet do it with gentleness and reverence.

4:   Keep your conscience clear, so that, when you are maligned, those who abuse you for your good conduct in Christ may be put to shame.

5:   For it is better to suffer for doing good, if suffering should be God's will, then to suffer for doing evil.

6:   For Christ also suffered for sins once for all, the righteous for the unrighteous, in order to bring you to God.
He was put to death in the flesh,

but made alive in the spirit,
in which also he went and made a proclamation to
the spirits in prison,
who in former times did not obey,
when God waited patiently in the days of Noah,
during the building of the ark,
in which a few, that is, eight persons,
were saved through water.

7: And baptism, which this prefigured, now saves you
— not as a removal of dirt from the body, but as
an appeal to God for a good conscience, through
the resurrection of Jesus Christ, who has gone into
heaven and is at the right hand of God, with angels,
authorities, and powers made subject to him.

Ascension
Psalm 47 (Psalm)
Clap Your Hands All You Peoples

Suggestions:
Use as a call to worship.
6 readers — youths
Read with vigor.
Invite the entire congregation to give a hand clap on signal by the readers at four times during the reading of this Psalm. Practice the first two lines together so each clap will fall in rhythm with the words. Tell the congregation that the second set of hand claps comes after the word, "Selah."

Key:
1 = boys
2 = girls

1   Clap your hands, all you peoples; *(clap)*

2:   shout to God with loud songs of joy. *(clap)*

1 and 2: For the Lord, the Most High, is awesome,
           a great king over all the earth.

1:   He subdued peoples under us,
           and nations under our feet.

2:   He chose our heritage for us,
           the pride of Jacob whom he loves.

(Speak "Selah" softly as a spoken pause.)
(2:)   Selah.

1:   God has gone up with a shout, *(clap)*

2:   The Lord with the sound of a trumpet. *(clap)*

1:	Sing praises to God,
All:	sing praises;
2:	sing praises to our King,
All:	sing praises.
	For God is the king of all the earth;
	sing praises with a psalm.
1:	God is king over the nations;
	God sits on his holy throne.
2:	The princes of the peoples gather
	as the people of the God of Abraham.
	For the shields of the earth belong to God;
	he is highly exalted.

Easter 7
Acts 1:6-14 (First Lesson)
Jesus Is Taken Up To Heaven

Suggestions:
Use as an anthem.
5 readers — 1 woman, 4 men of various ages

Key:
1 = storyteller
2 = disciple
3 = Jesus
4 and 5 = men in white

1:   So when [the Disciples] had come together, they asked him,

2:   "Lord, is this the time when you will restore the kingdom to Israel?"

1:   He replied,

3:   "It is not for you to know the times or periods that the Father has set by his own authority. But you will receive power when the Holy Spirit has come upon you; and you will be my witnesses in Jerusalem, in all Judea and Samaria, and to the ends of the earth."

1:   When he had said this, as they were watching, he was lifted up, and a cloud took him out of their sight. While he was going and they were gazing up toward heaven, suddenly two men in white robes stood by them. They said,

4:   "Men of Galilee, why do you stand looking up toward heaven?

5: This Jesus, who has been taken up from you into heaven, will come in the same way as you saw him go into heaven.''

1: Then they returned to Jerusalem from the mount called Olivet, which is near Jerusalem, a sabbath day's journey away. When they had entered the city, they went to the room upstairs where they were staying,

(1:) Peter, and John, and James, and Andrew, Philip and Thomas, Bartholomew and Matthew, James son of Alphaeus, and Simon the Zealot, and Judas son of James.

(1:) All these were constantly devoting themselves to prayer, together with certain women, including Mary the mother of Jesus, as well as his brothers.

Pentecost
Acts 2:1-21 (First Lesson)
The Coming Of The Holy Spirit

Suggestions:
Use as a call to worship or in ordinary sequence with the scripture reading.
Read with energy.
4 readers — 2 men and 2 women

Key:
1 = first storyteller
2 = second storyteller
3 = third storyteller
4 = Peter

1: When the day of Pentecost had come, they were all together in one place. And suddenly from heaven there came a sound like the rush of a violent wind, and it filled the entire house where they were sitting.

2: Divided tongues, as of fire, appeared among them, and a tongue rested on each of them. All of them were filled with the Holy Spirit and began to speak in other languages, as the Spirit gave them ability.

1: Now there were devout Jews from every nation under heaven living in Jerusalem. And at this sound the crowd gathered and was bewildered, because each one heard them speaking in the native language of each.

2: Amazed and astonished, they asked, "Are not all these who are speaking Galileans? And how is it that we hear, each of us, in our own native language?

3: Parthians, Medes, Elamites, and residents of Mesopotamia, Judea and Cappadocia, Pontus and Asia, Phrygia and Pamphylia, Egypt and the parts of Libya belonging to Cyrene, and visitors from Rome, both Jews and proselytes, Cretans and Arabs — in our own languages we hear them speaking about God's deeds of power.''

1: All were amazed and perplexed, saying to one another, ''What does this mean?''

3: But others sneered and said, ''They were filled with new wine.''

2: But Peter, standing with the 11, raised his voice and addressed them,

4: ''Men of Judea and all who live in Jerusalem, let this be known to you, and listen to what I say. Indeed, these are not drunk, as you suppose, for it is only nine o'clock in the morning.

(4:) No, this is what was spoken through the prophet Joel: 'In the last days it will be, God declares, that I will pour out my Spirit upon all flesh, and your sons and your daughters shall prophesy, and your young men shall see visions, and your old men shall dream dreams.

(4:) Even upon my slaves, both men and women, in those days I will pour out my Spirit; and they shall prophesy. And I will show portents in the heaven above and signs on the earth below, blood, and fire, and smoky mist.

(4:) The sun shall be turned to darkness and the moon to blood, before the coming of the Lord's great and glorious day. Then everyone who calls on the name of the Lord shall be saved.' ''

Trinity Sunday
Genesis 1:1—2:4a (First Lesson)
The Creation Story

Suggestions:
Use as an anthem.
6 readers — 2 junior high, 4 middle elementary youths
God is read in duet by girl & boy.
Encourage readers to read at a pace that does not drag.

Key:
1 and 2 = oldest readers
3 and 4 = easy reading
5 = boy comfortable with reading
6 = girl comfortable with reading

All: [In the beginning . . . .]

1:   In the beginning when God created the heavens and the earth,

2:   the earth was a formless void and darkness covered the face of the deep, while a wind from God swept over the face of the waters.

1:   Then God said,

5 and 6:   "Let there be light";

3:   and there was light.

4:   And God saw that the light was good;

2:   and God separated the light from the darkness. God called the light Day, and the darkness he called Night.

1: And there was evening and there was morning, the first day. And God said,

5 and 6: "Let there be a dome in the midst of the waters, and let it separate the waters from the waters."

2: So God made the dome and separated the waters that were under the dome from the waters that were above the dome.

3: And it was so.

2: God called the dome Sky.

1: And there was evening and there was morning, the second day. And God said,

5 and 6: "Let the waters under the sky be gathered together into one place, and let the dry land appear."

3: And it was so.

2: God called the dry land Earth, and the waters that were gathered together he called Seas.

4: And God saw that it was good.

1: Then God said,

5 and 6: "Let the earth put forth vegetation; plants yielding seed, and fruit trees of every kind on earth that bear fruit with the seed in it."

3: And it was so.

2: The earth brought forth vegetation: plants yielding seed of every kind, and trees of every kind bearing fruit with the seed in it.

4: And God saw that it was good.

1: And there was evening and there was morning, the third day. And God said,

5 and 6: "Let there be lights in the dome of the sky to separate the day from the night; and let them be for signs and for seasons and for days and years, and let them be lights in the dome of the sky to give light upon the earth."

3: And it was so.

1: God made the two great lights — the greater light to rule the day and the lesser light to rule the night — and the stars.

2: God set them in the dome of the sky to give light upon the earth, to rule over the day and over the night, and to separate the light from the darkness.

4: And God saw that it was good.

1: And there was evening and there was morning, the fourth day. And God said,

5 and 6: "Let the waters bring forth swarms of living creatures, and let birds fly above the earth across the dome of the sky."

2: So God created the great sea monsters and every living creature that moves, of every kind with which the waters swarm, and every winged bird of every kind.

4: And God saw that it was good.

1: God blessed them, saying,

5 and 6: "Be fruitful and multiply and fill the waters and the seas, and let birds multiply on the earth."

1: And there was evening and there was morning, the fifth day. And God said,

5 and 6: "Let the earth bring forth living creatures of every kind: cattle and creeping things and wild animals of the earth of every kind."

3: And it was so.

2: God made the wild animals of the earth of every kind, and the cattle of every kind, and everything that creeps upon the ground of every kind.

4: And God saw that it was good.

1: Then God said,

5 and 6: "Let us make humankind in our image, according to our likeness;
and let them have dominion over the fish of the sea,
and over the birds of the air,
and over the cattle,
and over all the wild animals of the earth,
and over every creeping thing that creeps upon the earth."

2: So God created humankind in his image, in the image of God he created them; male and female he created them.

1: God blessed them, and God said to them,

5 and 6: "Be fruitful and multiply,
and fill the earth and subdue it;

and have dominion over the fish of the sea
and over the birds of the air
and over every living thing that moves upon the
earth.''

1: God said,

5 and 6: "See, I have given you every plant yielding seed that
is upon the face of all the earth,
and every tree with seed in its fruit;
you shall have them for food.
And to every beast of the earth,
and to every bird of the air,
and to everything that creeps on the earth,
everything that has the breath of life,
I have given every green plant for food.''

3: And it was so.

1: God saw everything that he had made,

4: and indeed, it was very good.

1: And there was evening and there was morning, the
sixth day.

2: Thus the heavens and the earth were finished, and
all their multitude.

1: And on the seventh day God finished the work that
he had done, and he rested on the seventh day from
all the work that he had done. So God blessed the
seventh day and hallowed it, because on it God
rested from all the work that he had done in creation.

Proper 4
Psalm 46 (Psalm)
God Is Our Refuge And Strength

Suggestions:
Use before the pastoral prayer.
2 readers — senior spouses

Key:
1 = woman
2 = man

1: God is our refuge and strength,
a very present help in trouble.
Therefore we will not fear,
though the earth should change,

1 and 2: though the mountains shake in the heart of the sea;
though its waters roar and foam,
though the mountains tremble with its tumult.

(Speak "Selah" softly as a spoken pause.)
2: Selah.

(2:) There is a river whose streams make glad
the city of God,
the holy habitation of the most high.

1: God is in the midst of the city;
it shall not be moved;
God will help it when the morning dawns.

2: The nations are in an uproar,
the kingdoms totter;

1 and 2: he utters his voice,
the earth melts.
the Lord of hosts is with us;
the God of Jacob is our refuge.

95

2: Selah.

1: Come, behold the works of the Lord;
see what desolations he has brought on the earth.

2: He makes wars cease to the end of the earth;
he breaks the bow, and shatters the spear;
he burns the shields with fire.

1: "Be still, and know that I am God!
I am exalted among the nations,
I am exalted in the earth."

1 and 2: The Lord of hosts is with us;
the God of Jacob is our refuge.
Selah.

Proper 5
Matthew 9:9-13, 18-26 (Gospel)
Jesus Calls Matthew,
Jesus Heals The Leader's Daughter,
Jesus Heals The Hemorrhaging Woman

Suggestions:
Use as an anthem.
6 readers — 2 women, young man, 3 older men

Key:
1 = narrator
2 = Jesus
3 and 4 = Pharisees
5 = leader of the synagogue
6 = woman who hemorrhages

1:   As Jesus was walking along, he saw a man called Matthew sitting at the tax booth; and he said to him,

2:   "Follow me."

1:   And he got up and followed him.

1:   And as he sat at dinner in the house, many tax collectors and sinners came and were sitting with him and his disciples. When the Pharisees saw this, they said to his disciples,

3 and 4: "Why does your teacher eat with tax collectors and sinners?"

1:   But when he heard this, he said,

2:   "Those who are well have no need of a physician, but those who are sick. Go and learn what this means, 'I desire mercy, not sacrifice.' For I have come to call not the righteous but sinners."

1: While he was saying these things to them, suddenly a leader of the synagogue came in and knelt before him, saying,

5: "My daughter has just died; but come and lay your hand on her, and she will live."

1: And Jesus got up and followed him, with his disciples. Then suddenly a woman who had been suffering from hemorrhages for 12 years came up behind him and touched the fringe of his cloak, for she said to herself,

6: "If I only touch his cloak, I will be made well."

1: Jesus turned, and seeing her he said,

2: "Take heart, daughter; your faith has made you well."

1: And instantly the woman was made well. When Jesus came to the leader's house and saw the flute players and the crowd making a commotion, he said,

2: "Go away; for the girl is not dead but sleeping."

1: And they laughed at him. But when the crowd had been put outside, he went in and took her by the hand, and the girl got up. And the report of this spread throughout that district.

Proper 6
Genesis 18:1-15 (21:1-7) (First Lesson)
God Promises Abraham And Sarah A Son

Suggestions:
Use as an anthem.
* = optional stopping point
4 readers — 3 men, 1 woman

Key:
1 = storyteller
2 = Abraham
3 = person representing three men
4 = Sarah

1: The Lord appeared to Abraham by the oaks of Mamre, as he sat at the entrance of his tent in the heat of the day. He looked up and saw three men standing near him. When he saw them, he ran from the tent entrance to meet them, and bowed down to the ground. He said,

2: "My lord, if I find favor with you, do not pass by your servant. Let a little water be brought, and wash your feet, and rest yourselves under the tree. Let me bring a little bread, that you may refresh yourselves, and after that you may pass on — since you have come to your servant."

1: So they said,

3: "Do as you have said."

1: And Abraham hastened into the tent to Sarah, and said,

2: "Make ready quickly three measures of choice flour, knead it, and make cakes."

99

1:	Abraham ran to the herd, and took a calf, tender and good, and gave it to the servant, who hastened to prepare it. Then he took curds and milk and the calf that he had prepared, and set it before them; and he stood by them under the tree while they ate. They said to him,
3:	"Where is your wife Sarah?"
1:	And he said,
2:	"There, in the tent."
1:	Then one said,
3:	"I will surely return to you in due season, and your wife Sarah shall have a son."
1:	And Sarah was listening at the tent entrance behind him. Now Abraham and Sarah were old, advanced in age; it had ceased to be with Sarah after the manner of women. So Sarah laughed to herself, saying,
4:	"After I have grown old, and my husband is old, shall I have pleasure?"
1:	The Lord said to Abraham,
3:	"Why did Sarah laugh, and say, 'Shall I indeed bear a child, now that I am old?' Is anything too wonderful for the Lord? At the set time I will return to you, in due season, and Sarah shall have a son."
1:	But Sarah denied, saying,
4:	"I did not laugh";
1:	for she was afraid. He said,
3:	"Oh yes, you did laugh."

*

1: The Lord dealt with Sarah as he had said, and the Lord did for Sarah as he had promised. Sarah conceived and bore Abraham a son in his old age, at the time of which God had spoken to him. Abraham gave the name Isaac to his son whom Sarah bore him. And Abraham circumcised his son Isaac when he was eight days old, as God had commanded him. Abraham was a hundred years old when his son Isaac was born to him. Now Sarah said,

4 "God has brought laughter for me; everyone who hears will laugh with me."

1: And she said,

3: "Who would ever have said to Abraham that Sarah would nurse children? Yet I have borne him a son in his old age."

Proper 7
Genesis 21:8-21 (First Lesson)
Sarah Sends Away Hagar And Ishmael

Suggestions:
Use in ordinary sequence with the scripture reading.
4 readers — 2 men, 2 women

Key:
1 = first storyteller
2 = second storyteller
3 = Sarah
4 = God

1: [Isaac] the child [of Sarah and Abraham] grew, and was weaned; and Abraham made a great feast on the day that Isaac was weaned.

2: But Sarah saw the son of Hagar the Egyptian, whom she had borne to Abraham, playing with her son Isaac. So she said to Abraham,

3: "Cast out this slave woman with her son; for the son of this slave woman shall not inherit along with my son Isaac."

1: The matter was very distressing to Abraham on account of his son. But God said to Abraham,

4: "Do not be distressed because of the boy and because of your slave woman; whatever Sarah says to you, do as she tells you, for it is through Isaac that offspring shall be named for you. As for the son of the slave woman, I will make a nation of him also, because he is your offspring."

1: So Abraham rose early in the morning, and took bread and a skin of water, and gave it to Hagar, putting it on her shoulder, along with the child, and sent her away.

2: And she departed, and wandered about in the wilderness of Beer-sheba. When the water in the skin was gone, she cast the child under one of the bushes. Then she went and sat down opposite him a good way off, about the distance of a bowshot; for she said, "Do not let me look on the death of the child."

(2:) And as she sat opposite him, she lifted up her voice and wept. And God heard the voice of the boy; and the angel of God called to Hagar from heaven, and said to her,

4: "What troubles you, Hagar? Do not be afraid; for God has heard the voice of the boy where he is. Come, lift up the boy and hold him fast with your hand, for I will make a great nation of him."

2: Then God opened her eyes and she saw a well of water. She went, and filled the skin with water, and gave the boy a drink.

1: God was with the boy, and he grew up; he lived in the wilderness, and became an expert with the bow. He lived in the wilderness of Paran; and his mother got a wife for him from the land of Egypt.

Proper 8
Genesis 22:1-14 (First Lesson)
God Commands Abraham To Offer Isaac

Suggestions:
Use as an anthem.
4 readers — a woman as storyteller, a boy, a young man, an older man

Key:
1 = storyteller
2 = God
3 = Abraham
4 = Isaac

(Read the "he saids" quietly in a smooth rhythm with speakers to avoid monotony.)

1:   After [Abraham's agreement with Abimelech] God tested Abraham. He said to him,

2:   "Abraham!"

1:   And he said,

3:   "Here I am."

1:   He said,

2:   "Take your son, your only son Isaac, whom you love, and go to the land of Moriah, and offer him there as a burnt offering on one of the mountains that I shall show you."

1:   So Abraham rose early in the morning, saddled his donkey, and took two of his young men with him, and his son Isaac; he cut the wood for the burnt offering, and set out and went to the place in the distance that God had shown him. On the third day Abraham looked up and saw the place far away. Then Abraham said to his young men,

3: "Stay here with the donkey; the boy and I will go over there; we will worship, and then we will come back to you."

1: Abraham took the wood of the burnt offering and laid it on his son Isaac, and he himself carried the fire and the knife. So the two of them walked on together. Isaac said to his father Abraham,

4: "Father!"

1: And he said,

3: "Here I am, my son."

1: He said,

4: "The fire and the wood are here, but where is the lamb for a burnt offering?"

1: Abraham said,

3: "God himself will provide the lamb for a burnt offering, my son."

1: So the two of them walked on together. When they came to the place that God had shown him, Abraham built an altar there and laid the wood in order. He bound his son Isaac, and laid him on the altar, on top of the wood. Then Abraham reached out his hand and took the knife to kill his son. But the angel of the Lord called to him from heaven, and said,

2: "Abraham, Abraham!"

1: And he said,

3: "Here I am."

1: He said,

2: "Do not lay your hand on the boy or do anything to him; for now I know that you fear God, since you have not withheld your son, your only son, from me."

1: And Abraham looked up and saw a ram, caught in a thicket by its horns. Abraham went and took the ram and offered it up as a burnt offering instead of his son. So Abraham called that place "The Lord will provide"; as it is said to this day, "On the mount of the Lord it shall be provided."

Proper 9
Romans 7:15-25a (Second Lesson)
The Frustration Of Being Human

Suggestions:
Use in ordinary sequence with the scripture reading.
Speakers read in a thoughtful manner from a sitting position in their usual places in the pews.
9 readers — a variety of folk

Key:
1-9 = speakers

1: I do not understand my own actions. For I do not do what I want, but I do the very thing I hate.

2: Now if I do what I do not want, I agree that the law is good.

3: But in fact it is no longer I that do it, but sin that dwells within me.

4: For I know that nothing good dwells within me, that is, in my flesh.

5: I can will what is right, but I cannot do it.

6: For I do not do the good I want, but the evil I do not want is what I do.

7: Now if I do what I do not want, it is no longer I that do it, but sin that dwells within me.

8: So I find it to be a law that when I want to do what is good, evil lies close at hand.

9: For I delight in the law of God in my inmost self, but I see in my members another law at war with the law of my mind, making me captive to the law of sin that dwells in my members.

All: Wretched man that I am!
Who will rescue me from this body of death?
Thanks be to God through Jesus Christ our Lord!

Proper 10
Genesis 25:19-34 (First Lesson)
The Birth Of Esau and Jacob

Suggestions:
Use in ordinary sequence with the scripture readings.
5 readers — 2 female, 3 male

Key:
1 = storyteller
2 = Rebekah
3 = God
4 = Esau
5 = Jacob

1: These are the descendants of Isaac, Abraham's son: Abraham was the father of Isaac, and Isaac was 40 years old when he married Rebekah, daughter of Bethuel the Aramean of Paddan-aram, sister of Laban the Aramean.

(1:) Isaac prayed to the Lord for his wife, because she was barren; and the Lord granted his prayer, and his wife Rebekah conceived. The children struggled together within her; and she said,

2: "If it is to be this way, why do I live?"

1: So she went to inquire of the Lord. And the Lord said to her,

3: "Two nations are in your womb, and two peoples born of you shall be divided; the one shall be stronger than the other, the elder shall serve the younger."

1: When her time to give birth was at hand, there were twins in her womb. The first came out red, all his body like a hairy mantle; so they named him Esau. Afterward his brother came out, with his hand gripping Esau's heel; so he was named Jacob. Isaac was 60 years old when she bore them.

(1:) When the boys grew up, Esau was a skillful hunter, a man of the field, while Jacob was a quiet man, living in tents. Isaac loved Esau, because he was fond of game; but Rebekah loved Jacob.

(1:) Once when Jacob was cooking a stew, Esau came in from the field, and he was famished. Esau said to Jacob,

4: "Let me eat some of that red stuff, for I am famished!"

1: (Therefore he was called Edom.)
Jacob said.

5: "First sell me your birthright."

1: Esau said,

4: "I am about to die; of what use is a birthright to me?"

1: Jacob said,

5: "Swear to me first."

1: So he swore to him, and sold his birthright to Jacob. Then Jacob gave Esau bread and lentil stew, and he ate and drank, and rose and went his way. Thus Esau despised his birthright.

Proper 11
Genesis 28:10-19a (First Lesson)
Jacob's Dream At Bethel

Suggestions:
Use in ordinary sequence with the scripture readings.
4 readers — 2 older girls, 1 young man, 1 middle-aged man

Key:
1 = first storyteller
2 = second storyteller
3 = God
4 = Jacob

1:     Jacob left Beer-sheba and went toward Haran. He came to a certain place and stayed there for the night, because the sun had set. Taking one of the stones of the place, he put it under his head and lay down in that place. And he dreamed that there was a ladder set up on the earth, the top of it reaching to heaven; and the angels of God were ascending and descending on it.

2:     And the Lord stood beside him and said,

3:     "I am the Lord, the God of Abraham your father and the God of Isaac; the land on which you lie I will give to you and to your offspring; and your offspring shall be like the dust of the earth, and you shall spread abroad to the west and to the east and to the north and to the south; and all the families of the earth shall be blessed in you and in your offspring.

(3:)   Know that I am with you and will keep you wherever you go, and will bring you back to this land; for I will not leave you until I have done what I have promised you."

2: Then Jacob woke from his sleep and said,

4: "Surely the Lord is in this place — and I did not know it!"

2: And he was afraid, and said,

4: "How awesome is this place! This is none other than the house of God, and this is the gate of heaven."

1: So Jacob rose early in the morning, and he took the stone that he had put under his head and set it up for a pillar and poured oil on the top of it. He called that place Bethel.

Proper 12
Matthew 13:31-33, 44-52 (Gospel)
Kingdom Of Heaven Parables

Suggestions:
Use in ordinary sequence with the scripture readings.
6 readers — mixture of ages

Key:
1 = narrator
2 = male reader
3 = male reader
4 = female reader
5 = male reader
6 = female reader

1: [Jesus] put before them another parable:

2: "The kingdom of heaven is like a mustard seed that someone took and sowed in his field; it is the smallest of all the seeds, but when it has grown it is the greatest of shrubs and becomes a tree, so that the birds of the air come and make nests in its branches."

1: He told them another parable:

3: "The kingdom of heaven is like yeast that a woman took and mixed in with three measures of flour until all of it was leavened."

4: "The kingdom of heaven is like treasure hidden in a field, which someone found and hid; then in his joy he goes and sells all that he has and buys that field.

5: "Again, the kingdom of heaven is like a merchant in search of fine pearls; on finding one pearl of great value, he went and sold all that he had and bought it.

6: "Again, the kingdom of heaven is like a net that was thrown into the sea and caught fish of every kind; when it was full, they drew it ashore, sat down, and put the good into baskets but threw out the bad.

(6:) So it will be at the end of the age. The angels will come out and separate the evil from the righteous and throw them into the furnace of fire, where there will be weeping and gnashing of teeth.

2: "Have you understood all this?"

1: They answered, "Yes." And he said to them,

2: "Therefore every scribe who has been trained for the kingdom of heaven is like the master of a household who brings out of his treasure what is new and what is old."

Proper 13
Matthew 14:13-21 (Gospel)
Jesus Feeds The Five Thousand

Suggestions:
Use in ordinary sequence with the scripture readings.
4 readers — 1 young woman, 3 young men

Key:
1 = storyteller
2 and 4 = two disciples
3 = Jesus

1: Now when Jesus heard [the news about the death of John the Baptist], he withdrew from there in a boat to a deserted place by himself. But when the crowds heard it, they followed him on foot from the towns. When he went ashore, he saw a great crowd; and he had compassion for them and cured their sick. When it was evening, the disciples came to him and said,

2: "This is a deserted place, and the hour is now late; send the crowds away so that they may go into the villages and buy food for themselves."

1: Jesus said to them,

3: "They need not go away; you give them something to eat."

1: They replied,

4: "We have nothing here but five loaves and two fish."

1: And he said,

3: "Bring them here to me."

1: Then he ordered the crowds to sit down on the grass. Taking the five loaves and the two fish, he looked up to heaven, and blessed and broke the loaves, and gave them to the disciples, and the disciples gave them to the crowds. And all ate and were filled; and they took up what was left over of the broken pieces, 12 baskets full. And those who ate were about 5,000 men, besides women and children.

Proper 14
Genesis 37:1-4, 12-28 (First Lesson)
Joseph And His Brothers

Suggestions:
Use as an anthem.
8 readers — 3 women, 2 older men, 2 younger men, 1 youngest man
Let the three women read with the attentive attitude of three persons relating a story.
Let the storytellers read the "he saids" in smooth rhythm with the speakers to avoid monotony.
To offer contrast, let the storytellers read with engaging voices.

Key:
1, 2, 3 = women storytellers
4 = Israel (Jacob, the dad)
5 = Joseph
6 = man along the way
7 = Reuben (Joseph's oldest brother)
8 = Judah (Joseph's older brother)

1:   Jacob settled in the land where his father had lived as an alien, the land of Canaan. This is the story of the family of Jacob.

2:   Joseph, being 17 years old, was shepherding the flock with his brothers; he was a helper to the sons of Bilhah and Zilpah, his father's wives; and Joseph brought a bad report of them to their father.

3:   Now Israel loved Joseph more than any other of his children, because he was the son of his old age; and he had made him a long robe with sleeves.

2:   But when his brothers saw that their father loved him more than all his brothers, they hated him, and could not speak peaceably to him.

117

3:   Now his brothers went to pasture their father's flock near Shechem.

1:   And Israel said to Joseph,

4:   "Are not your brothers pasturing the flock at Shechem? Come, I will send you to them."

1:   He answered,

5:   "Here I am."

1:   So he said to him,

4:   "Go now, see if it is well with your brothers and with the flock; and bring word back to me."

1:   So he sent him from the valley of Hebron.

2:   He came to Shechem, and a man found him wandering in the fields; the man asked him,

6:   "What are you seeking?"

5:   "I am seeking my brothers,"

2:   he said;

5:   "tell me, please, where they are pasturing the flock."

2:   The man said,

6:   "They have gone away, for I heard them say, 'Let us go to Dothan.' "

2:   So Joseph went after his brothers, and found them at Dothan.

3: They saw him from a distance, and before he came near to them, they conspired to kill him. They said to one another, "Here comes this dreamer.

(3:) Come now, let us kill him and throw him into one of the pits; then we shall say that a wild animal has devoured him, and we shall see what will become of his dreams."

2: But when Reuben heard it, he delivered him out of their hands, saying,

7: "Let us not take his life."

2: Reuben said to them,

7: "Shed no blood; throw him into this pit here in the wilderness, but lay no hand on him"

2: — that he might rescue him out of their hand and restore him to his father.

3: So when Joseph came to his brothers, they stripped him of his robe, the long robe with sleeves that he wore; and they took him and threw him into a pit. The pit was empty; there was no water in it.

1: Then they sat down to eat; and looking up they saw a caravan of Ishmaelites coming from Gilead, with their camels carrying gum, balm, and resin, on their way to carry it down to Egypt.

3: Then Judah said to his brothers,

8: "What profit is it if we kill our brother and conceal his blood? Come, let us sell him to the Ishmaelites, and not lay our hands on him, for he is our brother, our own flesh."

3:   And his brothers agreed.

1:   When some Midianite traders passed by, they drew
Joseph up, lifting him out of the pit, and sold him
to the Ishmaelites for 20 pieces of silver. And they
took Joseph to Egypt.

Proper 15
Genesis 45:1-15 (First Lesson)
Joseph Reveals Himself To His Brothers

Suggestions:
Use as an anthem.
2 readers — mature person as storyteller, young man

Key:
1 = storyteller
2 = Joseph

1:   Then Joseph could no longer control himself before all those who stood by him, and he cried out,

2:   "Send everyone away from me."

1:   So no one stayed with him when Joseph made himself known to his brothers. And he wept so loudly that the Egyptians heard it, and the household of Pharaoh heard it. Joseph said to his brothers,

2:   "I am Joseph. Is my father still alive?"

1:   But his brothers could not answer him, so dismayed were they at his presence. Then Joseph said to his brothers,

2:   "Come closer to me."

1:   And they came closer. He said,

2:   "I am your brother, Joseph, whom you sold into Egypt. And now do not be distressed, or angry with yourselves, because you sold me here; for God sent me before you to preserve life.

(2:) For the famine has been in the land these two years; and there are five more years in which there will be neither plowing nor harvest.

(2:) God sent me before you to preserve for you a remnant on earth, and to keep alive for you many survivors.

(2:) So it was not you who sent me here, but God; he has made me a father to Pharaoh, and lord of all his house and ruler over all the land of Egypt. Hurry and go up to my father and say to him, 'Thus says your son Joseph, God has made me lord of all Egypt; come down to me, do not delay.

(2:) You shall settle in the land of Goshen, and you shall be near me, you and your children and your children's children, as well as your flocks, your herds, and all that you have.

(2:) I will provide for you there — since there are five more years of famine to come — so that you and your household, and all that you have, will not come to poverty.

(2:) And now your eyes and the eyes of my brother Benjamin see that it is my own mouth that speaks to you. You must tell my father how greatly I am honored in Egypt, and all that you have seen. Hurry and bring my father down here.''

1: Then he fell upon his brother Benjamin's neck and wept, while Benjamin wept upon his neck. And he kissed all his brothers and wept upon them; and after that his brothers talked with him.

Proper 16
Matthew 16:13-20 (Gospel)
Peter's Declaration About Jesus

Suggestions:
Use in ordinary sequence with the scripture readings.
7 readers — 1 woman, 6 young men
Peter speaks with hesitation.

Key:
1 = woman storyteller
2 = Jesus
3, 4, 5, 6 = disciples
7 = Peter

1:   Now when Jesus came into the district of Caesarea Philippi, he asked his disciples,

2:   "Who do people say that the Son of Man is?"

1:   And they said,

3:   "Some say John the Baptist,

4:   but others Elijah,

5:   and still others Jeremiah

6:   or one of the prophets."

1:   He said to them,

2:   "But who do you say that I am?"

1:   Simon Peter answered,

7:   "You are the Messiah, the Son of the living God."

1: And Jesus answered him,

2: "Blessed are you, Simon son of Jonah! For flesh and blood has not revealed this to you, but my Father in heaven. And I tell you, you are Peter, and on this rock I will build my church, and the gates of Hades will not prevail against it. I will give you the keys of the kingdom of heaven, and whatever you bind on earth will be bound in heaven, and whatever you loose on earth will be loosed in heaven."

1: Then he sternly ordered the disciples not to tell anyone that he was the Messiah.

Proper 17
Exodus 3:1-15 (First Lesson)
God Calls Moses

Suggestions:
Use as an anthem.
3 readers — 1 woman, 2 men (a tenor voice and a deeper voice)
The storyteller enables this story to move along by reading with
obvious interest.

Key:
1 = woman storyteller
2 = Moses
3 = God

1: Moses was keeping the flock of his father-in-law
Jethro, the priest of Midian; he led his flock beyond
the wilderness, and came to Horeb, the mountain
of God.

(1:) There the angel of the Lord appeared to him in a
flame of fire out of a bush; he looked, and the bush
was blazing, yet is was not consumed.

(1:) Then Moses said,

2: "I must turn aside and look at this great sight, and
see why the bush is not burned up."

1: When the Lord saw that he had turned aside to see,
God called to him out of the bush,

3: "Moses, Moses!"

1: And he said,

2: "Here I am."

1: Then he said,

3: "Come no closer! Remove the sandals from your feet, for the place on which you are standing is holy ground."

1: He said further,

3: "I am the God of your father, the God of Abraham, the God of Isaac, and the God of Jacob."

1: And Moses hid his face, for he was afraid to look at God.

1: Then the Lord said,

3: "I have observed the misery of my people who are in Egypt; I have heard their cry on account of their taskmasters.

(3:) Indeed, I know their sufferings, and I have come down to deliver them from the Egyptians, and to bring them up out of that land to a good and broad land, a land flowing with milk and honey, to the country of the Canaanites, the Hittites, the Amorites, the Perizzites, the Hivites, and the Jebusites.

(3:) The cry of the Israelites has now come to me; I have also seen how the Egyptians oppress them. So come, I will send you to Pharaoh to bring my people, the Israelites, out of Egypt."

1: But Moses said to God,

2: "Who am I that I should go to Pharaoh, and bring the Israelites out of Egypt?"

1: He said,

3: "I will be with you; and this shall be the sign for you that it is I who sent you: when you have brought the people out of Egypt, you shall worship God on this mountain."

1: But Moses said to God,

2: "If I come to the Israelites and say to them, 'The God of your ancestors has sent me to you,' and they ask me, 'What is his name?' what shall I say to them?"

1: God said to Moses,

3: "I am who I am."

1: He said further,

3: "Thus you shall say to the Israelites, 'I am has sent me to you.' "

1: God also said to Moses,

3: "Thus you shall say to the Israelites, 'The Lord, the God of your ancestors, the God of Abraham, the God of Isaac, and the God of Jacob, has sent me to you': This is my name forever, and this my title for all generations."

Proper 18
Romans 13:8-14 (Second Lesson)
Duties Toward Others

Suggestions:
Use in ordinary sequence with the scripture reading.
8 readers — a variety of folk
Speakers read in a frank manner from a sitting position in their usual places in the pews.

Key:
1-8 = speakers

1:        Owe no one anything, except to love one another; for the one who loves another has fulfilled the law.

2:        The commandments, "You shall not commit adultery; You shall not murder; You shall not steal; You shall not covet"; and any other commandment, are summed up in this word, "Love your neighbor as yourself."

3:        Love does no wrong to a neighbor; therefore, love is the fulfilling of the law.

4:        Besides this, you know what time it is, how it is now the moment for you to wake from sleep.

5:        For salvation is nearer to us now than when we became believers; the night is far gone, the day is near.

6:        Let us then lay aside the works of darkness and put on the armor of light;

7:   let us live honorably as in the day, not in reveling and drunkenness, not in debauchery and licentiousness, not in quarreling and jealousy.

8:   Instead, put on the Lord Jesus Christ, and make no provision for the flesh, to gratify its desires.

Proper 19
Exodus 14:19-31 (First Lesson)
Crossing The Red Sea (Or, The Sea Of Reeds)

Suggestions:
Use as an anthem.
4 readers — 2 men, 2 women

Key:
1 = first storyteller
2 = second storyteller
3 = third storyteller
4 = God

1:   The angel of God who was going before the Israelite army moved and went behind them; and the pillar of cloud moved from in front of them and took its place behind them.

(1:)   It came between the army of Egypt and the army of Israel. And so the cloud was there with the darkness, and it lit up the night; one did not come near the other all night.

2:   Then Moses stretched out his hand over the sea. The Lord drove the sea back by a strong east wind all night, and turned the sea into dry land; and the waters were divided. The Israelites went into the sea on dry ground, the waters forming a wall for them on their right and on their left.

3:   The Egyptians pursued, and went into the sea after them, all of Pharaoh's horses, chariots and chariot drivers. At the morning watch the Lord in the pillar of fire and cloud looked down upon the Egyptian army, and threw the Egyptian army into panic. He clogged their chariot wheels so that they turned with difficulty. The Egyptians said, "Let us flee from the Israelites, for the Lord is fighting for them against Egypt."

1: Then the Lord said to Moses,

4: "Stretch out your hand over the sea, so that the water may come back upon the Egyptians, upon their chariots and chariot drivers."

1: So Moses stretched out his hand over the sea, and at dawn the sea returned to its normal depth.

2: As the Egyptians fled before it, the Lord tossed the Egyptians into the sea. The waters returned and covered the chariots and the chariot drivers, the entire army of Pharaoh that had followed them into the sea; not one of them remained.

3: But the Israelites walked on dry ground through the sea, the waters forming a wall for them on their right and on their left.

1: Thus the Lord saved Israel that day from the Egyptians; and Israel saw the Egyptians dead on the seashore. Israel saw the great work that the Lord did against the Egyptians. So the people feared the Lord and believed in the Lord and in his servant Moses.

Proper 20
Matthew 20:1-16 (Gospel)
Parable Of The Workers In The Vineyard

Suggestions:
Use as an anthem.
5 readers — 1 woman, 2 mature men, 2 younger men

Key:
1 = male storyteller
2 = female storyteller
3 = vineyard owner
4 and 5 = two workers

1: "For the kingdom of heaven is like a landowner who went out early in the morning to hire laborers for his vineyard.

2: After agreeing with the laborers for the usual daily wage, he sent them into his vineyard. When he went out about nine o'clock, he saw others standing idle in the marketplace; and he said to them,

3: 'You also go into the vineyard, and I will pay you whatever is right.'

1: So they went.

2: When he went out again about noon and about three o'clock, he did the same. About five o'clock he went out and found others standing around; and he said to them,

3: 'Why are you standing here idle all day?'

1: They said to him,

4: 'Because no one has hired us.'

1: He said to them,

3: 'You also go into the vineyard.'

2: When evening came, the owner of the vineyard said to his manager,

3: 'Call the laborers and give them their pay, beginning with the last and going to the first.'

2: When those hired about five o'clock came, each of them received the usual daily wage.

1: Now when the first came, they thought they would receive more; but each of them also received the usual daily wage. And when they received it, they grumbled against the landowner, saying,

5: 'These last worked only one hour, and you have made them equal to us who have borne the burden of the day and the scorching heat.'

1: But he replied to one of them,

3: 'Friend, I am doing you no wrong; did you not agree with me for the usual daily wage? Take what belongs to you and go; I choose to give to this last the same as I give to you. Am I not allowed to do what I choose with what belongs to me? Or are you envious because I am generous?'

1: So the last will be first, and the first will be last.

Proper 21
Philippians 2:1-13 (Second Lesson)
Living Humbly

Suggestions:
Use in ordinary sequence with the scripture reading.
3 readers — adults

Key:
1 = first reader
2 = second reader
3 = third reader

1:   If then there is any encouragement in Christ,
any consolation from love,
any sharing in the Spirit,
any compassion and sympathy,
make my joy complete:

All: be of the same mind,
having the same love,
being in full accord and of one mind.

1:   Do nothing from selfish ambition or conceit, but in
humility regard others as better than yourselves.

2:   Let each of you look not to your own interests, but
to the interests of others.

3:   Let the same mind be in you that was in Christ Jesus,
who,
though he was in the form of God,
did not regard equality with God as something to
be exploited,
but emptied himself,
taking the form of a slave,
being born in human likeness.

2: And being found in human form,
he humbled himself and became obedient to the
point of death —
even death on a cross.

1: Therefore God also highly exalted him and gave him
the name that is above every name,

3: so that at the name of Jesus every knee should bend,
in heaven and on earth and under the earth,
and every tongue should confess that Jesus Christ
is Lord,
to the glory of God the Father.

1: Therefore, my beloved,
just as you have always obeyed me,
not only in my presence,
but much more now in my absence,
work out your own salvation with fear and
trembling;

All: for it is God who is at work in you,
enabling you both to will and to work for his good
pleasure.

Proper 22
Exodus 20:1-20 (First Lesson)
The Ten Commandments

Suggestions:
Use as an anthem.
6 readers — 3 women and 3 men of a variety of voice tones

Key:
1 = storyteller
2 = older woman
3 = younger woman
4 = older man
5 = younger man
6 = Moses

1:   Then God spoke all these words:

All: I am the Lord your God,

2:   who brought you out of the land of Egypt,

3:   out of the house of slavery;

All: you shall have no other gods before me.

All: You shall not make for yourself an idol,

2:   whether in the form of anything that is in heaven above,

3:   or that is on the earth beneath,

2 and 3: or that is in the water under the earth.

4: You shall not bow down to them or worship them; for I the Lord your God am a jealous God, punishing children for the iniquity of parents, to the third and the fourth generation of those who reject me,

5: but showing steadfast love to the thousandth generation of those who love me and keep my commandments.

All: You shall not make wrongful use of the name of the Lord your God,

2: for the Lord will not acquit anyone who misuses his name.

All: Remember the sabbath day, and keep it holy.

3: Six days you shall labor and do all your work.

4: But the seventh day is a sabbath to the Lord your God; you shall not do any work — you, your son or your daughter, your male or female slave, your livestock, or the alien residents in your towns.

3: For in six days the Lord made heaven and earth, the sea, and all that is in them, but rested the seventh day;

3 and 4: therefore the Lord blessed the sabbath day and consecrated it.

All: Honor your father and your mother,

5: so that your days may be long in the land that the Lord your God is giving you.

(Speak the next five commandments with a foot-beat pause after each.)

All: You shall not murder.

All: You shall not commit adultery.

All: You shall not steal.

All: You shall not bear false witness against your neighbor.

All: You shall not covet your neighbor's house;

2: you shall not covet your neighbor's wife or male or female slave, or ox, or donkey, or anything that belongs to your neighbor.

1: When all the people witnessed the thunder and lightning, the sound of the trumpet, and the mountain smoking, they were afraid and trembled and stood at a distance, and said to Moses,

Women: "You speak to us,
and we will listen;

Men: but do not let God speak to us,
or we will die."

1: Moses said to the people,

6: "Do not be afraid; for God has come only to test you and to put the fear of him upon you so that you do not sin."

Proper 23
Exodus 32:1-14 (First Lesson)
The Gold Calf

Suggestions:
Use as an anthem.
7 readers — 3 women, 2 young men, 2 older men
As Aaron is three years older than his brother Moses, let an older man with a deeper voice read Aaron's words.
Moses, tenor-voiced, should be a persuasive person.

Key:
1 = storyteller, a woman
2 = first person
3 = second person, a woman
4 = third person
5 = Aaron
6 = God, a man
7 = Moses

1: When the people saw that Moses delayed to come down from the mountain, the people gathered around Aaron, and said to him,

2: "Come, make gods for us, who shall go before us;

3: as for this Moses, the man who brought us up out of the land of Egypt,

4: we do not know what has become of him."

1: Aaron said to them,

5: "Take off the gold rings that are on the ears of your wives, your sons, and your daughters, and bring them to me."

139

1: So all the people took off the gold rings from their ears, and brought them to Aaron. He took the gold from them, formed it in a mold, and cast an image of a calf; and they said,

2, 3, 4: "These are your gods, O Israel, who brought you up out of the land of Egypt!"

1: When Aaron saw this, he built an altar before it; and Aaron made proclamation and said,

5: "Tomorrow shall be a festival to the Lord."

1: They rose early the next day, and offered burnt offerings and brought sacrifices of well-being; and the people sat down to eat and drink, and rose up to revel.

(1:) The Lord said to Moses,

6: "Go down at once! Your people, whom you brought up out of the land of Egypt, have acted perversely; they have been quick to turn aside from the way that I commanded them;

(6:) they have cast for themselves an image of a calf, and have worshiped it and sacrificed to it, and said, 'These are your gods, O Israel, who brought you up out of the land of Egypt!' "

1: The Lord said to Moses,

6: "I have seen this people, how stiff-necked they are. Now let me alone, so that my wrath may burn hot against them and I may consume them; and of you I will make a great nation."

1: But Moses implored the Lord his God, and said,

7: "O Lord, why does your wrath burn hot against your people, whom you brought out of the land of Egypt with great power and with a mighty hand? Why should the Egyptians say, 'It was with evil intent that he brought them out to kill them in the mountains, and to consume them from the face of the earth'?

(7:) Turn from your fierce wrath; change your mind and do not bring disaster on your people. Remember Abraham, Isaac and Israel, your servants, how you swore to them by your own self, saying to them, 'I will multiply your descendants like the stars of heaven, and all this land that I have promised I will give to your descendants, and they shall inherit it forever.' "

1: And the Lord changed his mind about the disaster that he planned to bring on his people.

Proper 24
Matthew 22:15-22 (Gospel)
The Question About Paying Taxes

Suggestions:
Use in ordinary sequence with the scripture readings.
6 readers — 1 young woman, 1 young man, 4 middle-aged and older men

Key:
1 — young woman storyteller
2, 3, 4, and 5 = men from oldest to youngest
6 = young man Jesus

1:   Then the Pharisees went and plotted to entrap him in what he said. So they sent their disciples to him, along with the Herodians, saying,

2:   "Teacher, we know that you are sincere, and teach the way of God in accordance with truth, and show deference to no one; for you do not regard people with partiality.

3:   Tell us, then, what you think.

4:   Is it lawful to pay taxes to the emperor,

5:   or not?"

1:   But Jesus, aware of their malice, said,

6:   "Why are you putting me to the test, you hypocrites? Show me the coin used for the tax."

1:   And they brought him a denarius. Then he said to them,

6:   "Whose head is this, and whose title?"

1: They answered,

2, 3, 4, 5: "The emperor's."

1: Then he said to them,

6: "Give therefore to the emperor the things that are the emperor's, and to God the things that are God's."

1: When they heard this, they were amazed; and they left him and went away.

Proper 25
Matthew 22:34-46 (Gospel Lesson)
The Two Commandments
And The Question About The Messiah

Suggestions:
Use in ordinary sequence with the scripture readings.
6 readers — 1 woman, 1 young man, 2 middle-aged men, 2 older men

Key:
1 = woman as storyteller
2 = lawyer
3 = young man as Jesus
4, 5 and 6 = other Pharisees

1: When the Pharisees heard that [Jesus] had silenced the Sadducees, they gathered together, and one of them, a lawyer, asked him a question to test him.

2: "Teacher, which commandment in the law is the greatest?"

1: He said to him,

3: " 'You shall love the Lord your God with all your heart, and with all your soul, and with all your mind.' This is the greatest and first commandment.

(3:) And a second is like it: 'You shall love your neighbor as yourself.' On these two commandments hang all the law and the prophets."

1: Now while the Pharisees were gathered together, Jesus asked them this question:

3: "What do you think of the Messiah? Whose son is he?"

144

1: They said to him,

2, 4, 5, 6: "The son of David."

1: He said to them,

3: "How is it then that David by the Spirit calls him Lord, saying, 'The Lord said to my Lord, "Sit at my right hand, until I put your enemies under your feet" '? If David thus calls him Lord, how can he be his son?"

1: No one was able to give him an answer, nor from that day did anyone dare to ask him any more questions.

Proper 26
Joshua 3:7-17 (First Lesson)
Carrying The Ark Of The Covenant
Across The Jordan

Suggestions:
Use in ordinary sequence with the scripture reading.
4 readers — 2 men, 2 women

Key:
1 = first storyteller
2 = Lord
3 = Joshua
4 = second storyteller

1: The Lord said to Joshua,

2: "This day I will begin to exalt you in the sight of all Israel, so that they may know that I will be with you as I was with Moses. You are the one who shall command the priests who bear the ark of the covenant, 'When you come to the edge of the waters of the Jordan, you shall stand still in the Jordan.' "

1: Joshua then said to the Israelites,

3: "Draw near and hear the words of the Lord your God."

1: Joshua said,

3: "By this you shall know that among you is the living God who without fail will drive out from before you the Canaanites, Hittites, Hivites, Perizzites, Girgashites, Amorites and Jebusites: the ark of the covenant of the Lord of all the earth is going to pass before you into the Jordan.

(3:)   So now select 12 men from the tribes of Israel, one from each tribe. When the soles of the feet of the priests who bear the ark of the Lord, the Lord of all the earth, rest in the waters of the Jordan, the waters of the Jordan flowing from above shall be cut off; they shall stand in a single heap.''

1:   When the people set out from their tents to cross over the Jordan, the priests bearing the ark of the covenant were in front of the people.

4:   Now the Jordan overflows all its banks throughout the time of harvest. So when those who bore the ark had come to the Jordan, and the feet of the priests bearing the ark were dipped in the edge of the water, the waters flowing from above stood still, rising up in a single heap far off at Adam, the city that is beside Zarethan, while those flowing toward the sea of Arabah, the Dead Sea, were wholly cut off.

3:   Then the people crossed over opposite Jericho. While all Israel were crossing over on dry ground, the priests who bore the ark of the covenant of the Lord stood on dry ground in the middle of the Jordan, until the entire nation finished crossing over the Jordan.

All Saints' Sunday
Matthew 5:1-12 (Gospel Lesson)
The Beatitudes

Suggestions:
Use as an anthem or before the pastoral prayer.
8 readers — 4th through 7th graders

Key:
From 1 to 8 with number 1 the youngest

All: When Jesus saw the crowds, he went up the mountain;
and after he sat down, his disciples came to him.
Then he began to speak, and taught them, saying:

1: "Blessed are the poor in spirit,

All: for theirs is the kingdom of heaven.

4: "Blessed are those who mourn,

All: for they will be comforted.

2: "Blessed are the meek,

All: for they will inherit the earth.

5: "Blessed are those who hunger and thirst for righteousness,

All: for they will be filled.

3: "Blessed are the merciful,

All: for they will receive mercy.

8:   "Blessed are the pure in heart,

All: for they will see God.

6:   "Blessed are the peacemakers,

All: for they will be called children of God.

7:   "Blessed are those who are persecuted for righteousness' sake,

All: for theirs is the kingdom of heaven.

8:   "Blessed are you, when people revile you and persecute you and utter all kinds of evil against you falsely on my account.

All: Rejoice and be glad, for your reward is great in heaven, for in the same way they persecuted the prophets who were before you."

Proper 27
Matthew 25:1-13 (Gospel)
Parable Of The Ten Bridesmaids

Suggestions:
Use as an anthem.
5 readers — 2 older women, 1 young man, 2 young women

Key:
1 = narrator
2 = voice in the night
3 = a foolish bridesmaid
4 = a wise bridesmaid
5 = bridegroom

1: "Then the kingdom of heaven will be like this. Ten bridesmaids took their lamps and went to meet the bridegroom. Five of them were foolish, and five were wise.

(1:) When the foolish took their lamps, they took no oil with them; but the wise took flasks of oil with their lamps. As the bridegroom was delayed, all of them became drowsy and slept. But at midnight there was a shout,

2: 'Look! Here is the bridegroom! Come out to meet him!

1: Then all those bridesmaids got up and trimmed their lamps. The foolish said to the wise,

3: 'Give us some of your oil, for our lamps are going out!'

1: But the wise replied,

4:   'No! there will not be enough for you and for us; you had better go to the dealers and buy some for yourselves.'

1:   And while they went to buy it, the bridegroom came, and those who were ready went with him into the wedding banquet; and the door was shut. Later the other bridesmaids came also, saying,

3:   'Lord, Lord, open to us.'

1:   But he replied,

5:   'Truly I tell you, I do not know you.'

1:   Keep awake therefore, for you know neither the day nor the hour.''

Proper 28
Matthew 25:14-30 (Gospel)
The Parable Of The Talents

Suggestions:
Use as an anthem.
Tell in storytelling fashion.
5 readers — 1 older man as storyteller, 1 middle-aged man, 3 younger men

Key:
1 = main storyteller
2, 3 and 4 = men given talents
5 = master

1: "For it is as if a man, going on a journey, summoned his slaves and entrusted his property to them;

2: to one he gave five talents,

3: to another two,

4: to another one,

1: to each according to his ability. Then he went away.

2: The one who had received the five talents went off at once and traded with them, and made five more talents.

3: In the same way, the one who had two talents made two more talents.

4: But the one who had received the one talent went off and dug a hole in the ground and hid his master's money.

1: After a long time the master of those slaves came and settled accounts with them.

2: Then the one who had received the five talents came forward, bringing five more talents, saying, 'Master, you handed over to me five talents; see, I have made five more talents.'

5: His master said to him, 'Well done, good and trustworthy slave; you have been trustworthy in a few things, I will put you in charge of many things; enter into the joy of your master.'

3: And the one with the two talents also came forward, saying, 'Master, you handed over to me two talents; see, I have made two more talents.'

5: His master said to him, 'Well done, good and trustworthy slave; you have been trustworthy in a few things, I will put you in charge of many things; enter into the joy of your master.'

4: Then the one who had received the one talent also came forward, saying, 'Master, I knew that you were a harsh man, reaping where you did not sow, and gathering where you did not scatter seed; so I was afraid, and I went and hid your talent in the ground. Here you have what is yours.'

5: But his master replied, 'You wicked and lazy slave! You knew, did you, that I reap where I did not sow, and gather where I did not scatter? Then you ought to have invested my money with the bankers, and on my return I would have received what was my own with interest.

(5:) So take the talent from him, and give it to the one with the ten talents. For to all those who have, more will be given, and they will have an abundance; but from those who have nothing, even what they have will be taken away. As for this worthless slave, throw him into the outer darkness, where there will be weeping and gnashing of teeth.' ''

Christid The King
Matthew 25:31-46 (Gospel)
The Final Judgment

Suggestions:
Use as an anthem.
8 readers — 1 older woman, 1 young man, 3 boys and girls who enjoy reading, 3 middle-aged adults

Key:
1 = older woman
2 = Jesus
3, 4 and 7 = boys and girls
5, 6 and 8 = adults

1: "When the Son of Man comes in his glory, and all the angels with him, then he will sit on the throne of his glory. All the nations will be gathered before him,

(1:) and he will separate people one from another as a shepherd separates the sheep from the goats, and he will put the sheep at his right hand and the goats at the left. Then the king will say to those at his right hand,

2: 'Come, you that are blessed by my Father, inherit the kingdom prepared for you from the foundation of the world;

3: for I was hungry and you gave me food,

4: I was thirsty and you gave me something to drink,

5: I was a stranger and you welcomed me,

6: I was naked and you gave me clothing,

7: I was sick and you took care of me,

8: I was in prison and you visited me.'

1: Then the righteous will answer him,

4 and 5: 'Lord, when was it that we saw you hungry and gave you food, or thirsty and gave you something to drink?

5 and 6: And when was it that we saw you a stranger and welcomed you?

6 and 7: or naked and gave you clothing?

7 and 8: And when was it that we saw you sick or in prison and visited you?'

1: And the king will answer them,

2: 'Truly I tell you, just as you did it to one of the least of these who are members of my family, you did it to me.'

1: Then he will say to those at his left hand,

2: 'You that are accursed, depart from me into the eternal fire prepared for the devil and his angels; for I was hungry and you gave me no food,

(2:) I was thirsty and you gave me nothing to drink, I was a stranger and you did not welcome me, naked and you did not give me clothing, sick and in prison and you did not visit me.'

1: Then they also will answer,

4 thru 8: 'Lord, when was it that we saw you hungry
or thirsty
or a stranger
or naked
or sick
or in prison, and did not take care of you?'

1: Then he will answer them,

8: 'Truly I tell you, just as you did not do it to one of the least of these, you did not do it to me.'

1: And these will go away into eternal punishment, but the righteous into eternal life.''

Thanksgiving Sunday, USA
Psalm 65 (Psalm)
Praise Is Due You, O God

Suggestions:
Use as a call to worship.
9 readers — three-generational groups of men

Key:
1 = 3 fathers
2 = 3 grandfathers
3 = 3 sons

1: Praise is due to you, O God, in Zion;
and to you shall vows be performed,
O you who answer prayer!

2: To you all flesh shall come.
When deeds of iniquity overwhelm us,
you forgive our transgressions.

1: Happy are those whom you choose and bring near
to live in your courts.
We shall be satisfied with the goodness of your
house, your holy temple.

3: By awesome deeds you answer us with deliverance,
O God of our salvation;
you are the hope of all the ends of the earth and
of the farthest seas.

2: By your strength you established the mountains;
you are girded with might.
You silence the roaring of the seas,
the roaring of their waves,
the tumult of the peoples.

1: Those who live at earth's farthest bounds are awed by your signs;
you make the gateways of the morning and the evening shout for joy.

3: You visit the earth and water it,
you greatly enrich it;
the river of God is full of water;
you provide the people with grain,
for so you have prepared it.

2: You water its furrows abundantly,
settling its ridges,
softening it with showers,
and blessing its growth.

3: You crown the year with your bounty;
your wagon tracks overflow with richness.

All: The pastures of the wilderness overflow,
the hills gird themselves with joy,
the meadows clothe themselves with flocks,
the valleys deck themselves with grain,
they shout and sing together for joy.

Pronunciation Guide

Key: Emphasize capitalized syllables

A

Aaron (AIR•un)
Abimelech (a•BIM•e•lek)
Alphaeus (al•FEE•us)
Amorites (AM•or•rights)
Arabah (ARE•a•ba)
Arabs (AIR•abz)
Aramean (AIR•a•MAY•an)
Archelaus (are•ke•LAY•us)
Ascension (a•SEN•shun)

B

Balaam (BAY•lam)
Balak (BAY•luck)
Bartholomew (bar•THOW•lo•mew)
Bashan (BAY•shan)
Beer-sheba (beer•SHE•ba)
Beor (BEE•or)
Bethel (BETH•el)
Bethuel (be•THU•el)
Bilah (BILL•ha)

C

Canaan (KAY•nan)
Canaanites (KAY•nan•nights)
Cappadocia (cap•a•DOE•she•ah)
Carmel (CAR•mell)
Caesarea Philippi (ses•sa•RE•ah)
Colossians (co•LOS•shens)
Cretans (CRE•tans)
Cyrene (si•REEN)

D

Denarius (den•AIR•e•us)
Dothan (DO•than)

E

Edom (E•dom)
Egypt (E•gypped)
Elamites (ELAM•mights)
Elijah (e•LIE•jah)
Ephah (F•ah)
Epiphany (E•PIF•a•knee)
Epistle (E•PIS•el)
Esau (E•SAW)
Ezekiel (E•Z•key•l)
Exodus (X•O•dus)

G

Galileans (gal•i•LEE•anz)
Galilee (GAL•i•LEE)
Genesis (GEN•e•sis)
Gilead (GILL•e•add)
Gilgal (GILL•GALL)
Girgashites (GIR•ga•shites)
Goshen (GO•shen)

H

Hades (HEY•dee•z)
Hager (HEY•gar)
Haran (HEY•ran)
Hebron (HE•brun)
Herod (HAIR•ud)
Herodians (he•ROW•dee•anz)
Hittites (HIT•TIGHTS)
Hivites (HI•vitz)
Horeb (HO•reb)
hyssop (HISS•op)

I

Isaac (EYE•zak)

Isaiah (eye•ZAY•ah)
Ishmael (ISH•may•el)
Ishmaelites (ISH•ma•lights)
Israel (IZ•ray•el)

J

Jebusites (JEB•you•sights)
Jericho (JERRY•ko)
Jerusalem (je•RU•sa•lem)
Jesse (JES•see)
Jews (JEWS)
Jethro (JE•throw)
Joel (JOE•el)
Judah (JEW•dah)
Judas (JEW•does)
Judea (jew•DEE•ah)

L

Laban (LAY•ban)
Lebanon (LEB•a•non)
Libya (LIBBY•ya)

M

Mamre (MAM•ra)
Medes (MEEDS)
Midian (MID•e•an)
Midianite (MID•e•an•night)
Mesopotamia (mess•oh•Poe•tame•e•ah)
Messiah (mess•SIGH•ah)
Micah (MIKE•ah)
Miriam (MIR•e•am)
Moab (MOW•AB)
Moriah (more•EYE•ah)
Moses (MOW•zus)

N

Nazareth (NAZ•are•eth)
Nazorean (naz•or•E•an)
Noah (NO•AH)

O

Olivet (oli•VET)

P

Paddan-aram (PAD•dan AIR•ram)
Pamphylia (pam•FEEL•Lee•ah)
Paran (PAY•ran)
Parthians (PAR•thi•anz)
Pentecost (PENT•i•cost)
Perizzites (PAIR•i•zites)
Pharaoh (FARE•oh)
Pharisees (FARE•i•seas)
Philippians (fi•LIP•ianz)
Phrygia (FRIG•e•ah)
Pontus (PONT•us)
Prophesy (prof•e•sigh)
Psalm (SALM)

R

Rabbi (RAB•bye)
Ramah (RAH•ma)
Rebekah (re•BECK•ka)
Reuben (RU•ben)
Rome (ROAM)

S

Sadducees (SAD•you•sees)
Samaria (sah•MARY•ah)
Selah (SAY•LA)
Sheba (SHE•ba)
Shechem (SHE•come)
Shittim (SHIT•im)
Siloam (si•LOW•am)
Sychar (SIGH•car)

Z

Zarethan (ZAR•e•than)
Zealot (ZELL•lut)
Zilpah (ZIL•pa)
Zion (ZI•ON)

Scripture Index

Cast Of Speakers

Advent 1 — 2 readers — father and son
Advent 2 — 2 readers — a couple
Advent 3 — 6 readers — women of various ages
Advent 4 — 3 readers — women from three generations
Christmas Eve/Day — 3 readers — women from three generations
Christmas 1 — 4 readers — 2 older women as storytellers, 2 middle-aged men
Christmas 2 — 5 readers — women
Epiphany — 2 readers — men whose voice strengths are similar
Epiphany 1 — 4 readers — men
Epiphany 2 — 4 readers — women
Epiphany 3 — 2 readers — a mature couple
Epiphany 4 — 4 readers — 2 men and 2 women
Epiphany 5 — 2 readers — 2 men or 2 women
Epiphany 6 — 9 readers — a variety of folk
Epiphany 7 — 3 readers — women with serenity
Epiphany 8 — 10 readers — men and women of all ages
Transfiguration Sunday — 4 readers — 2 men and 2 women
Ash Wednesday — 14 readers — a variety of folk
Lent 1 — 3 readers — 1 younger woman, 1 older woman, 1 young man
Lent 2 — 2 readers — senior spouses
Lent 3 — 4 readers — 2 women, 2 men (second storyteller should have a soft voice)
Lent 4 — 5 readers — 1 woman as storyteller, 4 men
Lent 5 — 2 readers — men with strong voices
Palm Sunday — 3 readers — all women
Monday of Holy Week — 4 readers — a combination of two or three generations
Tuesday of Holy Week — 4 readers — a combination of two or three generations
Wednesday of Holy Week — 4 readers — a combination of two or three generations
Maundy Thursday — 4 readers — a combination of two or three generations
Good Friday — 4 readers — a combination of two or three generations

169

Holy Saturday — 4 readers — a combination of two or three generations

Easter — 2 readers — 2 men

Easter 2 — 4 readers — 2 long-married couples

Easter 3 — 3 readers — men or women

Easter 4 — 6 readers — males spanning three generations

Easter 5 — 4 readers — 3 boys and 1 girl

Easter 6 — 7 readers — various ages

Ascension Of The Lord — 6 readers — youths

Easter 7 — 5 readers — 1 woman, 4 men of various ages

Day Of Pentecost — 4 readers — 2 men and 2 women

Trinity Sunday — 6 readers — 2 junior high and 4 middle elementary youths

Proper 4 — 2 readers — senior spouses

Proper 5 — 6 readers — 2 women, young man, 3 older men

Proper 6 — 4 readers — 3 men, 1 woman

Proper 7 — 4 readers — 2 men, 2 women

Proper 8 — 4 readers — a woman as storyteller, a boy, a young man, an older man

Proper 9 — 9 readers — a variety of folk

Proper 10 — 5 readers — 2 female, 3 male

Proper 11 — 4 readers — 2 older girls, 1 young man, 1 middle-aged man

Proper 12 — 6 readers — a mixture of ages

Proper 13 — 4 readers — 1 young woman, 3 young men

Proper 14 — 8 readers — 3 women, 2 older men, 2 younger men, 1 youngest man

Proper 15 — 2 readers — mature person as storyteller, young man

Proper 16 — 7 readers — 1 woman, 6 young men

Proper 17 — 3 readers — 1 woman, 2 men (a tenor voice and a deeper voice)

Proper 18 — 8 readers — a variety of folk

Proper 19 — 4 readers — 2 men, 2 women

Proper 20 — 5 readers — 1 woman, 2 mature men, 2 younger men

Proper 21 — 3 readers — adults

Proper 22 — 6 readers — 3 women and 3 men of a variety of voice tones

Proper 23 — 7 readers — 3 women, 2 young men, 2 older men

Proper 24 — 6 readers — 1 young woman, 1 young man, 4 middle-aged and older men

Proper 25 — 6 readers — 1 woman, 1 young man, 2 middle-aged men, 2 older men

Proper 26 — 4 readers — 2 men, 2 women

All Saints' Day — 8 readers — 4th through 7th graders

Proper 27 — 5 readers — 2 older women, 1 young man, 2 young women

Proper 28 — 5 readers — 1 older man as storyteller, 1 middle-aged man, 3 younger men

Christ The King — 8 readers — 1 older woman, 1 young man, 3 boys and girls who enjoy reading, 3 middle-aged adults

Thanksgiving Day, USA — 9 readers — three-generational groups of men